Nero

Blackwell Ancient Lives

At a time when much scholarly writing on the ancient world is abstract and analytical, this series presents engaging, accessible accounts of the most influential figures of antiquity. It re-peoples the ancient landscape; and while never losing sight of the vast gulf that separates antiquity from our own world, it seeks to communicate the delight of reading historical narratives to discover "what happened next."

Published

Nero
Jürgen Malitz

Tiberius
Robin Seager

King Hammurabi of Babylon
Marc Van De Mieroop

Pompey the Great
Robin Seager

Age of Augustus
Werner Eck

Hannibal
Serge Lancel

In Preparation

Cleopatra
Sally Ann-Ashton

Constantine the Great
Timothy Barnes

Pericles
Charles Hamilton

Julius Caesar
W. Jeffrey Tatum

Alexander the Great in His World
Carol Thomas

Nero

Jürgen Malitz

Translated by Allison Brown

Blackwell
Publishing

BLACKWELL PUBLISHING
350 Main Street, Malden, MA 02148-5020, USA
9600 Garsington Road, Oxford OX4 2DQ, UK
550 Swanston Street, Carlton, Victoria 3053, Australia

First published by Verlag C.H. Beck in 1999 under the title *Nero*
English translation published 2005 by Blackwell Publishing Ltd

1   2005

Library of Congress Cataloging-in-Publication Data

Malitz, Jürgen.
  [Nero. English]
  Nero / Jürgen Malitz (trans. by Allison Brown).
    p. cm. — (Blackwell ancient lives)
  Includes bibliographical references and index.
  ISBN-13: 978-1-4051-2177-4 (hard cover : alk. paper)
  ISBN-10: 1-4051-2177-7 (hard cover : alk. paper)
  ISBN-13: 978-1-4051-2178-1 (pbk. : alk. paper)
  ISBN-10: 1-4051-2178-5 (pbk. : alk. paper)
    1. Nero, Emperor of Rome, 37–68. 2. Emperors—Rome—
Biography. 3. Rome—History—Nero, 54–68. I. Title. II. Series.

DG285.M3513 2005
937'.07'092—dc22

                                                            2004027395

A catalogue record for this title is available from the British Library.

Picture research by Kitty Bocking
Set in 10.5/13pt Trump Mediaeval
by Graphicraft Limited, Hong Kong
Printed and bound in the United Kingdom
by TJ International Ltd, Padstow, Cornwall

The publisher's policy is to use permanent paper from mills that operate a sustainable forestry policy, and which has been manufactured from pulp processed using acid-free and elementary chlorine-free practices. Furthermore, the publisher ensures that the text paper and cover board used have met acceptable environmental accreditation standards.

For further information on
Blackwell Publishing, visit our website:
www.blackwellpublishing.com

Contents

Illustrations

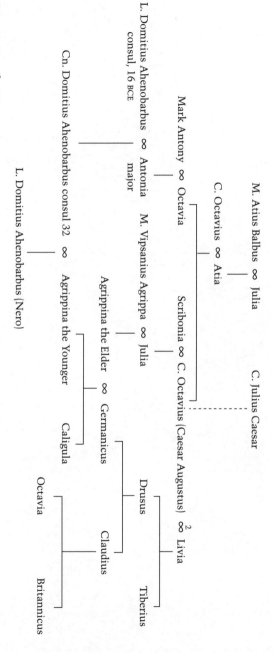

Nero's Family Tree

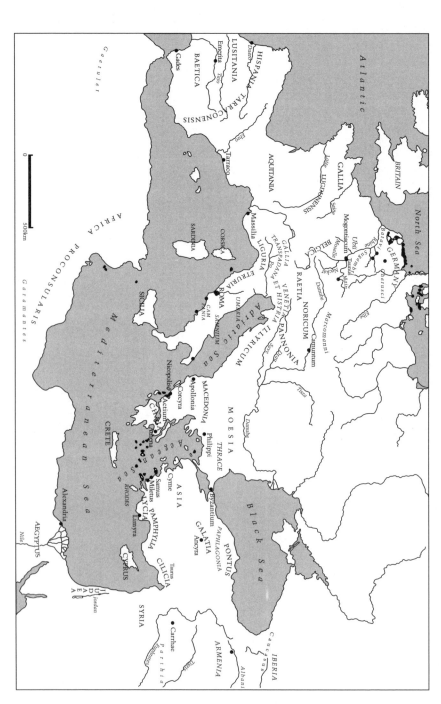

The Roman Empire

Timeline

37   Nero (until the year 50 his name is officially Lucius Domitius Ahenobarbus) is born as the son of Gnaeus Domitius Ahenobarbus and Julia Agrippina (twenty-three years old at the time) in Antium (December 15).

37–41   Reign of Caligula.

41–54   Reign of Claudius.

49   Claudius marries his niece Agrippina. Seneca becomes Nero's tutor. Nero performs in public for the first time. Nero is engaged to Octavia (about ten years old), daughter of Claudius.

50   Claudius adopts Nero (February 25).

51   Nero comes of age, a year earlier than is usual. He speaks before the Senate.

53   Nero marries Octavia. The Parthians invade Armenia.

54   Claudius dies (October 13). Nero is named princeps. His advisors are Burrus and Seneca. His "policy statement" is well received. Agrippina has Junius Silanus murdered since he is a rival. The Parthians occupy Armenia. Corbulo is appointed commander-in-chief in the eastern provinces.

55   Britannicus dies. Seneca publishes *De clementia*. Agrippina is stripped of her power. Nero falls in love with the freedwoman Acte.

56   Nero's nightly escapades in Rome. Senatorial debate on secondary issues is viewed as a sign of a new liberality.

57   A new amphitheater is built. Generous gift of money (*congiarium*) to the people of Rome.

58   Nero supports impoverished senators. Corbulo disciplines the troops before starting his campaign and then conquers Artaxata, the capital of Armenia. Nero receives decrees of honor. Nero declines opportunity to be a consul for life. Seneca is attacked. Poppaea Sabina becomes Nero's lover. Thrasea Paetus enters the Senate.

59   Agrippina is murdered. Nero's first semi-public performances as a singing kithara player and charioteer at the *Juvenalia* games. Corbulo conquers Tigranocerta in Armenia.

60   Corbulo installs Tigranes as king of Armenia. The "*Neronia*" games are held. Rubellius Plautus is exiled as an alleged rival.

61   Revolt of Boudicca in Britain.

62   The *maiestas* law (high treason law) is reinstituted. Burrus dies. Faenius Rufus and Ofonius Tigellinus command the praetorian guard. Seneca withdraws from public life. Cornelius Sulla is executed as a rival in Massilia, as is Rubellius Plautus in Asia Minor. Nero gets divorced from Octavia and she is executed shortly thereafter (June 9). Nero marries Poppaea Sabina. Praetorian prefect Ofonius Tigellinus has a growing influence on Nero. New fighting ensues against the Parthians after Tigranes is driven out.

63   Birth of Nero's daughter Claudia Augusta, who dies a few months later.

64   Nero performs publicly as a kitharode in Naples for the first time. Sudden postponement of his planned trip to Greece. The Great Fire of Rome (July 18–19). Christians are executed as alleged

arsonists. The city of Rome is rebuilt. Construction begins on Nero's new palace complex (*Domus Aurea*).

65   Pisonian conspiracy. Nero orders Seneca's death. Nymphidius Sabinus becomes the second commander of the praetorians. Poppaea dies.

66   Thrasea Paetus is tried and commits suicide. Nero marries Statilia Messalina. King Tiridates of Armenia pays homage to Nero in Rome and receives his diadem from Nero's hand. The revolt in Judaea begins. Nero begins his travels to Greece in September.

67   Nero participates in the panhellenic games and receives 1,808 prizes. Construction of the Isthmus Canal begins. Corbulo commits suicide in Corinth. Vespasian is sent to Judaea. On November 28, Nero "frees" Greece of having to pay taxes and grants them self-administration. Campaigns in Georgia and Ethiopia are presumably planned.

68   Nero returns to Italy ahead of schedule. On March 20, in Naples, Nero receives first news of the revolt by Gaius Julius Vindex in Gaul. On April 2, Galba is proclaimed imperator by his troops in Spain. In May news arrives of Verginius Rufus' victory over Vindex. On July 9, the Senate declares Galba to be the new princeps. Nero dies on June 9 or shortly thereafter.

I

Augustus' Great-great-grandson

Nero, the future emperor, was born on December 15, 37. In addition to his parents, the ruling princeps Gaius Caligula was also in attendance at his formal naming ceremony nine days later. The infant's father, Domitius Ahenobarbus, was evidently no longer in the best of health; in any case his mother Agrippina had requested that her brother Caligula give the baby boy a name. Caligula was somewhat consternated by the birth of a boy who by virtue of his descent from Caesar Augustus, the idolized founder of the dynasty, would in future provide inspiration for the gossip in the capital. Caligula was always good for what could be very cynical jokes at someone else's expense, and so he made reference to his uncle Claudius, who had always been the one to live out the existence of a droll but unavoidable family member at the court. Yes, the boy should receive his name. Everyone understood the princeps' intention if the child received either Claudius' first name Tiberius or his cognomen Nero. With this suggestion Caligula wanted to make it clear that his young nephew would have just as little prospects of succeeding him as his aging uncle did.

But Agrippina's son, in the tradition of his father's family and without consideration for the emperor's wit, was named Lucius Domitius Ahenobarbus. He would later be adopted by Claudius and become his heir.

Agrippina, twenty-one or twenty-two at the time, was the daughter of one of the most popular princes of the ruling house, Nero Claudius Drusus, with the cognomen Germanicus. He had died suddenly at thirty-four, in the year 19, while on a diplomatic mission in the eastern part of the empire. Marriages within the Roman aristocracy were carefully arranged; at the behest of Tiberius, Gnaeus Domitius Ahenobarbus, the infant's father, had been married to the then thirteen-year-old Agrippina in the year 28. Through his line of descent from Augustus' sister, he was a great-nephew of the princeps and was thus considered an appropriate partner for the young girl, who was herself a great-granddaughter of Augustus. The family of the Domitii was one of the supporting pillars of Augustan rule. During the civil war the grandfather of the groom had gone over to the victorious side in time; the father proved himself as a successful and even loyal commander on the German front. In his last will and testament Augustus named him to be one of the executors of the will. And so the wedding between his son and Agrippina could be regarded virtually as a belated reward for family service to the ruling house. Tiberius had him elected consul in the year 32.

Agrippina was indeed an excellent match for any aristocrat. She was the daughter of Germanicus and Agrippina the Elder and was among the closest relatives of the ruling family. Her father, Nero Claudius Drusus, was a great-nephew of the first princeps through his grandmother Octavia. He had not only assumed his cognomen Germanicus from his father Drusus, the popular stepson of Augustus, but had earned it himself in campaigns in Germany. His charisma was undisputed and he was a cultured man, very open especially to the Greek civilization. In the public memory his merits were elevated even higher through his early death, regarded by many as mysterious. Agrippina's mother was also named Agrippina. It was a new female name within the great families of Rome, and chosen with great self-confidence. Nero was the great-grandson of Julia, the only daughter of Augustus. Julia was married to Marcus Vipsanius Agrippa, the most important liege of the emperor for many years though he was only of the equestrian order. And so Caligula's malicious joke becomes understandable: Agrippina's son, irrespective of his individual talents, had to be closely watched in all matters concerning succession.

Nero's ancient critics saw his parents as having certain traits that could have set the course he would eventually take. Agrippina, who gave birth to the boy after almost ten years of marriage, must have already been unusually power-conscious back then. She was raised in the belief that her father Germanicus was robbed of his rightly entitled succession when he was poisoned, supposedly on orders of Tiberius. Her mother, Germanicus' widow, and two of her brothers lost their lives in the course of the intrigues of Tiberius' praetorian prefect Sejanus. Her brother Caligula was spared the same fate in the nick of time through intervention by Tiberius.

The biographer Suetonius wrote that the paternal ancestors of Nero had already demonstrated some of the unpleasant characteristics of the ruler. His grandfather enjoyed horrendous gladiator games so much that he was reprimanded by Augustus, and his father was considered irascible and brutal. Both of them, as Suetonius noted, enjoyed chariot races and theater performances to a degree not befitting their position.

Nothing except for her marriage in the year 28 is known about Agrippina's life before the birth of her son. Irrespective of the fate of her parents, her husband Domitius offered her – despite considerable family wealth – perhaps fewer political prospects than she had originally envisioned. At the end of Tiberius' rule, Domitius got caught up in a political affair that could have cost him his life if Tiberius had not died in the year 37. Barely escaping a catastrophe, Domitius left no further traces in the subsequent years until his death in the year 40. If his comments about the birth of his son are not authentic, then they were well invented: "Nothing that was not abominable and a public bane could be born of Agrippina and himself." (Suet., *Nero*, 6.1)

In the first two years of the reign of her brother Caligula, Agrippina – together with her two sisters Drusilla and Julia Livilla – played the role she was assigned as a lady of the ruling house. The sisters received the honorable rights of vestal virgins, and the usual oath of the soldiers and magistrates to the ruler was modified to include the welfare of the sisters.

And yet a full year before the death of Domitius, Agrippina's life in the capital ended in a scandal. The death of Caligula's favorite sister Drusilla hit him especially hard and it is possible that the two surviving sisters, Agrippina and Julia Livilla, did not pay sufficient attention to the mistrust of their quick-tempered brother. Very soon afterward he suspected his brother-in-law Marcus Aemilius Lepidus, also a distant relative of Augustus, to be a dangerous rival. Agrippina was accused of adultery with her brother-in-law and forced to carry the urn with the ashes of her executed alleged lover from the site of his arrest to Rome. Caligula did not leave anything up to chance, and banished both his sisters to a bleak Mediterranean island. It is impossible to confirm whether or not there was any truth to the accusations against Agrippina, enriched with severe suspicions of a sexual nature quite in the style of the day. In any case it cannot be ruled out that even before the death of Domitius Agrippina would use any means possible to ensure that her son, and indirectly herself, would have some prospects of power. The alleged lover Lepidus could have become Nero's legal guardian.

Nero, almost four years old at the time, was cheated out of his inheritance by Caligula. He had placed Nero in the care of his aunt Domitia Lepida, the sister of his father. In the house of this incredibly wealthy lady who was, however, known for her stinginess, the boy would be raised under very wretched conditions. As long as Caligula remained alive, this great-great-grandson of Augustus would have no prospects of attaining a position befitting his status.

II

Heir to the Throne

Nero did not have to live with his aunt for very long. Caligula was murdered on January 24, 41. The praetorians did not give the senate all that much time for debate and instead declared Claudius to be the new princeps. The public was surprised, but Claudius had always been a member of the court and, after all those years of hurt feelings, he was filled with ambition. The praetorian guards saw that he was the only one who would be in a position to satisfy all the material demands of the bodyguard, and that was enough of an argument for them to declare him imperator. And the senate had to follow suit.

Agrippina was allowed to travel home, where she regained her fortune and her son. She immediately sought a new husband in order to increase her influence. The cautious Galba, who was to succeed Nero in the year 68, evaded Agrippina's advances. Instead, the very wealthy and influential Gaius Sallustius Passienus Crispus became her husband for a few years (until 47). His will served to benefit Agrippina and her son. And so it is not surprising that not everyone was convinced her spouse died of natural causes.

Agrippina was successful in her efforts to gain the favor of the new ruler, who was the brother of Germanicus and thus also her uncle. An early example of her endeavors to make sure the public did not forget her son is the careful preparation of Nero's performance when the noble youths acted out the battle of Troy on the occasion of the secular games organized by Claudius in the year 47. The great-great-grandson of Augustus received thunderous applause, more than the ruling princeps' own son, Britannicus, who was three years younger. Claudius did not pay much attention to such performances, even if they were detrimental to his son. Claudius' wife Valeria Messalina, Britannicus' mother, reacted differently. She recognized Agrippina as a threat to Britannicus' future.

Messalina was killed hardly a year later on orders of Claudius. Ancient reports speak of an odd marriage ceremony between Messalina and Gaius Silius, who was known as the most handsome of all Romans. All the tolerance of the princeps notwithstanding, this forced him to act. Messalina was regarded as sexually insatiable, but this *amour fou* could have been part of a political plan to bring the rule of the disputed Claudius to a premature end. C. Silius would then have become Britannicus' guardian. The loyal advisors had a hard time convincing Claudius of the necessity to let Messalina die as a traitor.

The widower's preferences for marital cohabitation were known throughout the city, despite his obvious enjoyment of more common ladies of the court, so he quickly became the plaything of the aristocratic family policies. Agrippina, with the support of the powerful freedman Pallas, had overcome all rivals and persuaded Claudius to marry her. This was not a matter of course since the closeness of the relations of uncle and niece was considered an obstacle to marriage. This traditional regulation was revoked through a well-orchestrated decision by the Senate. It was not only the attractive niece herself, however, that might have persuaded the almost sixty-year-old Claudius to enter into matrimony. Just as attractive was the notion that it would be in his own interest to keep Agrippina's ambitions under control. No other man should have the chance to become Nero's stepfather.

With her marriage in early 49, Agrippina had attained a position that no reasonable augur or astrologer would have dared to prophesy a year earlier. She had put an impressive

Figure 1 Nero as a child. The bulla around his neck shows that he is still a minor. akg-images/Erich Lessing

amount of energy into building up her court status and from the outset she led the struggle for Nero's future with extreme ruthlessness. His position was already bettered by plans for his marriage to the ten-year-old Octavia, daughter of Claudius. Octavia had been engaged to marry Lucius Junius Silanus, also a great-great-grandson of Augustus and therefore satisfying the basic conditions for consideration in questions of succession. Agrippina won over Lucius

Vitellius, one of the ruler's most influential advisors, for her plans. Young Silanus was charged with incest with his sister and expelled from the Senate. His suicide on Agrippina's wedding day was certainly not an admission of guilt. Instead, it was a final attempt to save the family wealth from being confiscated, which would have accompanied the inevitable verdict of guilty. Since a sufficient number of senators were informed of Agrippina's plans, she was able to push through a senatorial decision demanding Claudius to entrust his daughter to the young Lucius Domitius Ahenobarbus.

Rome's public was well aware of the consequences of promoting Agrippina's son like that. And whoever Agrippina used for her own purposes knew even better. She did not limit herself to winning over reliable followers in the Senate and around the praetorian camp. Her decision not to entrust the education of her then thirteen-year-old son to just any of the renowned teachers (often not freeborn), as was otherwise common in aristocratic households, showed considerable foresight. Instead she sent for one of the best-known intellectuals in the capital, who was also a member of the Senate.

In the year 49, Agrippina declared Lucius Annaeus Seneca to be the young prince's tutor. The two Greek home teachers were almost meaningless in comparison. Seneca had a strong sense of gratitude toward Agrippina (which he never spoke or wrote about, for reasons of discretion); and he felt nothing but extremely unphilosophical hatred for Claudius. The ambitious philosopher and esthete came from a knightly family in Spain. In the year 41, during the reign of Caligula, he fell victim to a court intrigue. The asthmatic scholar was barely spared the death penalty as an alleged lover of Julia Livilla; since then he had had to endure life in exile in Corsica, totally devoid of the intellectual stimulation of the capital. All petitions for pardon, even at the cost of total self-denial, had failed. In the end Agrippina managed to get Claudius not only to pardon him, but also to award the returnee a praetorship. She also appointed him as the prince's tutor. Of course he knew very well what was expected of him: very little philosophy instruction, since there were Greek teachers available for that. Instead he was to educate the boy to be an eloquent orator, rhetorician, and – when the time was right – heir to the throne.

It was not enough for Agrippina simply to have made plans for the conscientious education of her son. A decisive step was her push for Claudius to adopt Nero, which he did on February 25, 50, although the ruler also had a healthy legitimate son. He might have justified this step by virtue of remotely comparable precedents set during the late reign of Augustus, with whom any comparison would be regarded as flattering. Nero's full name became Tiberius Claudius Nero Caesar or Nero Claudius Caesar Drusus Germanicus. He was three years older than Claudius' own son Britannicus. Quite in line with Agrippina's wishes, Claudius supported his adoptive son in a manner that certainly surprised political observers. Based on the model of preparations for earlier successions under Augustus and Tiberius, Claudius' actions seemed to designate Nero, rather than his own son, as heir apparent.

The fostering of Nero by his stepfather corresponded to how Agrippina appeared in the public eye. Within the context of Nero's adoption, Agrippina was given the honorary name "Augusta" by senatorial decree. This honor had not officially been given to Livia, wife of Augustus, until after her death. And it was nothing short of sensational when Agrippina's portrait was minted on the obverse side of imperial coins, signalizing that Claudius' new wife had gained considerable clout in the court in a short amount of time.

In the year 51 Nero already received the *toga virilis* as a sign of having reached adulthood. He was only thirteen years old at the time, so this was one year earlier than usual. The distinctions mounted up. He was named *princeps juventutis*, was admitted into the great priestly colleges, and in the year 57, when he was nineteen, he was designated as consul, also earlier than usual practice. Finally,

Figure 2   Agrippina. Vatican Museums, Galleria Chiaramonti

the authority that was considered an unmistakable sign of his prospects for the succession was conferred upon him: the proconsular authority over all provinces of the empire. The coins minted in those years made it even clearer to the public, in Rome and beyond, that Claudius preferred Nero over his own son to be his successor.

Claudius, who spent the long years prior to his appointment as princeps conducting historical studies, evidently did not grasp the consequences of promoting Nero ahead of Britannicus. When Nero reached legal age in the year 51, the event was also used to let him appear during Circus games in triumphal robes next to Britannicus, who was dressed in a child's toga. On the basis of age alone this served to emphasize Britannicus' secondary status.

Having adult status, Nero was permitted to appear before the Senate, where he could put to the test his rhetorical skills as Seneca had taught him. Immediately following the first honorary decrees the fourteen-year-old expressed his gratitude in an inspiring speech that was certainly composed with Seneca's help. A year later he demonstrated filial piety by swearing an oath before the Senate that he would hold Games once the ill ruler had convalesced.

In 53, after Nero married the unhappy Octavia, the time had come for a more sophisticated speech in the Senate. His oratorical exercise went far back into ancient history on the relations between Troy, the homeland of Aeneas, and Rome, which had been founded by Aeneas' descendants. In the end the Senate granted the petition to strike all taxes, as had been agreed upon beforehand. Nero appeared more than once in this style as a benefactor for indebted communities. The city of Bononia (Bologna) received a financial subvention following a fire; the people of Rhodes regained their freedom; and Syrian Apamea, which had been devastated by an earthquake, received a five-year remission of taxes on petition of the prince. Such speeches allowed Nero not only to demonstrate the progress of Seneca's instruction; he also gained the favor of the cities he helped.

Although the people of Rome could be manipulated to offer storms of applause for Nero, this was certainly only a segment of the populace. There were still people at the court who held alive the memory of Britannicus out of sheer fear of Agrippina. Nero's own aunt, Domitia Lepida, with whom he was forced to spend a few meager months shortly before Caligula's death, was also Messalina's mother and thus Britannicus' grandmother. Her attempts to gain influence over Nero stirred the suspicions of Agrippina and led to charges against her for alleged magical attacks on Agrippina and disruption of the public order through poorly supervised slaves.

Lepida's death was a further sign of the power struggle between Agrippina and her adversaries at court, whose aims she was well aware of. The day Britannicus came of age was an important moment for his supporters. In February 55, on his fourteenth birthday, he would receive the *toga virilis.* Claudius seemed meanwhile to have become aware of his error in ostracizing Britannicus. But the coming-of-age celebration never took place. Claudius died on October 13, 54, supposedly of mushroom poisoning, and this death fit into Agrippina's plans so perfectly that conjectures that he had been murdered by poison are understandable. Inexplicable deaths easily invited such speculation in antiquity, though this was of course impossible to verify. If it was not an assassination through poison, but indeed only mushroom poisoning (though Claudius seemed to be the only one at the table who fell ill), then the doctors of choice called in by Agrippina would have done little to help him. And at precisely that time Claudius' loyal freedman Narcissus had been sent away on convalescent leave.

The hours in which the princeps was wrestling with death were used to arrange the succession. Negotiations had to be completed quickly, all the more if Claudius' mushroom poisoning was to look like an accident. Claudius had prepared a will, of course, in which he commented on the future roles of Nero and Britannicus. But the will was not read, on orders of Agrippina. There is every reason to believe that son and stepson received equal treatment, just as Tiberius did in his last will and testament, in which his grandson Tiberius Gemellus and his great-nephew Caligula were treated equally.

Ever since the precedent set when Claudius was named princeps, the most important factor was reaching agreement among the praetorian guards. Agrippina had already arranged in 51 that Sextus Afranius Burrus replaced the two praetorian prefects and received sole charge. He had been distinguished as an officer but even more so through his many years as procurator in imperial service. Burrus received his advancement solely due to Agrippina, but at the same time he lacked any extreme personal ambition and his competence and straightforwardness were absolutely unquestionable.

Around noon on October 13, 54, when the streets of Rome were not overly crowded, seventeen-year-old Nero, together with Burrus, approached the praetorians on duty. The prefect told them what was expected of them, and Nero was greeted by resounding applause. He was brought by litter into the praetorian camp, where the young man gave a speech that was appropriate under the circumstances. It was received well, if only because he promised each guard the handsome sum of 15,000 sesterces, that is, five years' salary. Following this agreement he was proclaimed imperator. A short time later the Senate confirmed the praetorians' decision and passed all resolutions required for Nero's authorization.

This smooth transfer of power cannot be explained by good orchestration alone. The speedy acceptance of the seventeen-year-old was ultimately possible because many senators decidedly disliked the arbitrary regime of the aging Claudius. His mixture of learned absent-mindedness and bizarre cruelty in recent years had made him unbearable to senators and officers alike.

Agrippina had prepared her son well to accede to the throne. Caesar's heir Octavian, who later became Augustus, had only been slightly older when he accepted the testament of Caesar in 44 BCE and took on the battle against his enemies with a clarity and discipline that were astounding for his age.

It is impossible to say for sure whether Agrippina truly felt her son of the difficult father Domitius was capable of ruling. For her, it was not only a matter of her son's status. She obviously also thought about possessing a piece of the power, if only indirectly, that as a woman she could never have had – in Rome – in her own name. When Nero later had to justify the murder of his mother he claimed that in the year 54 Agrippina had toyed with the idea of appearing before the praetorians herself. Her enemies at least certainly did not consider this accusation to be totally ungrounded.

The extant evidence of Nero's youth is all colored by knowledge of what later developed. For example, there is not a single piece of information about Nero prior to 54 that made it possible to assume that the young man might have had any merits that spoke for his being heir to the highest position of power other than the burning ambition of his mother and the fact that he was related to Augustus.

Nero grew up totally under the influence of this unscrupulously ambitious mother. He never contradicted her will of iron, but some evidence suggests at least in retrospect that he sometimes tried to avoid overly excessive demands. Seneca took care of educating him in all the subjects that were necessary for a future princeps, or actually for any young aristocrat. His mother made sure that his philosophy lessons remained limited, presumably out of worry that high-flown philosophical ideas could make the young man lose interest in the position intended for him. Maybe Agrippina occasionally felt that her son's ambitions were not as directed toward the highest public office as she would have liked. Nero's pronounced interest in poetry, painting, and acting did not contradict his standing in principle; but it was another question whether he would have the strength to subordinate such leanings to the traditional role of a Roman aristocrat.

The praetorians and the Senate accepted Nero as heir to the throne. The military had been won over through money and their memories of Nero's grandfather Germanicus. Most of the senators were happy to see the end of Claudius' regime and, because Nero was a descendant of Augustus, they could accept him based on usual dynastic considerations alone. For one thing, Seneca and Burrus were the most influential men around Nero and they guaranteed a beneficial rejection of everything that had made Claudius so unpopular in the preceding years. And the young ruler had also shown the populace that he understood the signs of the times: the first motto that the new commander in chief gave to his guards was: The Best of Mothers (*"Optima Mater"*).

III

Quinquennium Neronis

The well-planned transfer of power to the seventeen-year-old Nero shows how completely the political order created by Augustus had asserted itself within only a few decades. Not a single realistic senator at that time would have even considered disputing Nero's position. The legitimacy of the ruler through his relationship to Augustus was too binding. Agrippina assessed the situation similarly; only a short time after Nero was proclaimed imperator she engaged two devoted henchmen in Asia Minor to poison the governing proconsul Junius Silanus. Presumably she made official reference to secret orders of the young princeps. The only "offense" committed by the man, who was regarded as harmless (Caligula had ridiculed him as a "golden sheep"), was the fact that he was Augustus' great-great-grandson, exactly the same relationship to Augustus as Nero's.

Those around Nero did not see it as a major challenge that the ruling authority lay in the hands of a very young princeps not overly interested in current political affairs. The "role" of the ruler had been so clearly laid out by Augustus and his descendants that disinterest or inappropriate behavior of a descendant did not immediately cause the system to collapse. The vast majority of senators had long since come to terms with the "monarchy." Consequently, Caligula, who in his final two years had rarely missed an opportunity to provoke the senatorial order in political matters, was killed not by assassins from the

Senate, but by a praetorian officer whom he undiplomatic-ally offended personally on numerous occasions. All the more secure was the position of the inexperienced Nero, as long as he kept to the suggestions of his able advisors who knew what mattered.

The first speech that Seneca had prepared for Nero to make before the Senate sounded very promising. Nero spoke about the advantage of his young years which enabled him to rule without taking up old hostilities, and about his intention to follow good advice and orient himself toward the model set by Augustus. When Nero became more spe-cific, it was always about eliminating the ills of the previ-ous regime. Claudius' intimidating enjoyment in personally administering justice was to become a thing of the past and, something the Senate wanted to hear, the embarrassing influence of "ministers" from the class of freedmen was to end. Finally, in contrast to his predecessor the young ruler promised to respect the traditional authority of the Senate, a highly welcomed announcement for most senators.

Agrippina's unbridled ambition surely added an element of uncertainty. One of Nero's first coins showed Agrippina on the obverse side, which usually depicted a portrait of the ruler. Another very unusual honor granted by the Senate directly after Claudius' death was the right to two officers, or lictors, who preceded Agrippina at public appearances. Up to then only magistrates and the *Vestalis Maxima*, or chief vestal virgin, had the right to such attendants.

On top of that, Agrippina left no stone unturned trying to expand her position in the initial months of Nero's rule, showing no regard whatsoever for her son's reputation. Burrus and Seneca, who owed their present positions to Agrippina, faced a difficult task. Tacitus reported on Seneca's diplomatic masterpiece in avoiding a disgrace in foreign policy. At the start of an audience that Nero had granted an Armenian delegation, Agrippina made a move to sit next to Nero on the platform, which was her way of demon-strating her equal partaking of power. While everyone else froze with horror and did not dare to undertake anything to

Figure 3   Nero and Agrippina: Aureus, circa 54–55 CE. Left, the bust of the young Nero; right, the bust of his mother. The legend for Agrippina is on the obverse side of the coin, shown here; it therefore gives the impression that the emperor's mother could have requested such a minting on her own: Agripp(ina) Aug(usta) divi Claud(I uxor) Neronis Caes(aris) mater. Hirmer Fotoarchiv

save the situation, Seneca had the presence of mind to tell Nero to rise and greet his mother and then graciously show her to a suitable seat in the background. Nero followed the good advice.

The first five years of Nero's reign were characterized by the later emperor Trajan as a model chapter in Roman history, as the "*Quinquennium Neronis.*" Trajan's criteria in making such a statement, and the historical – and possibly apologetic – tradition he was thereby adopting, are disputed in specifics. But there can be no doubt that these initial years of Nero's rule were definitely esteemed by the senatorial aristocracy, since it was primarily the senators who determined how history was passed down, and their criteria for a "good" ruler are apparent. The greater the authority – in the capital, in Italy, in the provinces – delegated to the Senate, the more the princeps could reckon with senatorial support. There was nothing innovative about the details of the aforementioned "policy statement" of the young ruler. Caligula and Claudius had made similar statements at the start of their reigns, but they both soon forgot their good intentions. Nero on the other hand kept to his "policy statement" for several years and allowed the senators the – often minimal – rights and competencies they felt were intrinsically significant for their institution.

Tacitus, whose *Annals* contain a report on the early years, emphasized the well-meaning attention that Nero (and his advisors) paid to all issues involving the Senate. He gave examples of Nero's policies that were welcomed by the Senate, the relatively minor relevance of which serves to underscore how little true authority the Senate retained. Merely relieving the quaestors of the costly obligation of holding gladiator games in the capital during their year of service was praised as a sign of the greatest goodwill. Even a pale reflection of republican debates between officials was enough for the senators to feel some of their old significance and they were content if the princeps did not intervene in these "senatorial" matters.

They wanted to demonstrate their independence, but they also gladly accepted favors from the emperor. It was lauded as proof of profound imperial respect for the Senate when in the year 58 Nero contributed to the assets of three impoverished senators such that they satisfied the necessary census. It is therefore understandable that it by no means contradicted the self-image of the Senate when the senators surprised the princeps with flattering petitions whenever the opportunity arose. There were also careerists who exposed the emperor to the danger of compromising himself if he accepted such honors, such as the petition to start the Roman calendar in December, the month of the ruler's birth. One petition that Nero "modestly" rejected at first, but later accepted, awarded him the title "father of the fatherland," though he was still young in years. Gestures of pointed restraint that did not cost anything politically were just as important for the posthumous fame of the *Quinquennium Neronis*, as were concrete political decisions that favored some expansion of the Senate's competence area.

The relaxed domestic situation during Nero's initial reigning years is also apparent from the coins that were minted. The SC (*ex senatus consulto* – by decree of the senate) proclaimed during this time on gold and silver coins should not be understood as an indication of senatorial authorization of the corresponding precious metal coinage, but as an acknowledgment by the emperor that he owed the honors formulated through his form of address to the Senate.

What share of the good *Quinquennium Neronis* was due to Nero himself? Ancient sources make it difficult to determine whether Nero had any direct influence on political dealings in the early years of his reign at all, or whether he relied on his advisors and experts in order to free up more leisure time for himself. Very little political farsightedness can be identified in Nero's actions during the *Quinquennium Neronis*. If any imperial initiatives during the initial years can be mentioned explicitly as personal decisions, then it was well-meant but incompetent notions such as abolishing taxes in the year 58. It required some expert consultations to withdraw the proposal. Decisions that can be shown to have been made by Nero himself were usually highly problematic, such as his dispatching of the freedman Polyclitus in 61 (that is, after the quinquennium) to enforce his policies in the state of Britain. Whenever developments were crisis-laden in his later years and he had to make a decision on his own, Nero panicked. As long as Burrus and Seneca remained unchallenged as his advisors, Nero's ideas did not cause any damage. Even those who were envious could not deny that the two of them in mutual agreement assured the smooth operation of government affairs, until at the latest when Burrus died in 62.

Burrus held an official position as praetorian prefect and would have advised Nero especially on matters of military security. Seneca was the emperor's personal advisor and primarily responsible for setting up his political guidelines. Never before had an advisor of a princeps exercised such influence. Among the descendants of Augustus, Nero was the first who noticeably had his public addresses formulated in advance, at least in his early years.

Seneca attached great importance to the public perception of his role as tutor (*educator*) and advisor (*amicus*). In his treatise published in 55 "On Clemency" (*De clementia*), not only did he address his young charge as his tutor, he also let the literary public know the standards by which he proposed to educate and advise the ruler.

It is nevertheless difficult to find documented traces of Seneca's activities in the contemporary political affairs. Especially as regards decisions that could be presumed to have been of personal interest to him as a philosopher from Spain – such as regarding the law of slavery or provincial administration – there is no indication of his direct influence whatsoever. In the year 55 Seneca was even a consul for three months. For neither this time nor the other years was Seneca ever mentioned as a participant in the sessions of the Senate, although everyone would have attached great importance to his opinion. He evidently avoided taking part in important sessions precisely for that reason. Nero also never ordered him to appear before the Senate, perhaps wanting the sessions thereby to appear more liberal, without the presence of someone who might report to the princeps. Even Seneca's works that were written after he had withdrawn from the public arena lack any reference to his many years as the most significant advisor to the ruler.

Seneca always valued living according to the sophisticated moral criteria of the Stoics. He often must have felt greatly torn in accomplishing his tasks. The aforementioned treatise "On Clemency" was presumably published after the death of Britannicus. Seneca might have been among those who considered the violent death of a potential successor to the throne to be justifiable if it served the avoidance of a civil war. Another example of the enormous moral conflicts that Seneca faced in his role at court was his participation in the "crisis management" following Agrippina's murder. While he saw the impending disaster in the offing, he was not informed of preparations for the deed. But he was in fact present when Nero gave the direct order for the murder and, on Nero's instructions, he wrote the declaration to be read before the Senate on the details of the alleged assassination plans of Agrippina and on her death. Any senators familiar with Seneca's style of writing knew immediately that the emperor himself had not written the report.

In retrospect it is easy to criticize Seneca's concessions to court reality and his own ambition. Without a doubt he was at the mercy of fault-finding fellow philosophers when he brought Stoic teachings – according to which he tried to live – into consonance with the intrigues of the imperial court. Seneca was proud of having remained true to the core of his philosophical beliefs, as was apparent from his private conversations with Nero in which he tried to the best of his knowledge and belief to do justice to his task as tutor. Tacitus, who had an unerring eye for any hypocrisy or self-deception, regarded Seneca fundamentally as a sincere and conscientious man, albeit sometimes somewhat vain and also rich.

The later notion of an exemplary quinquennium during the first five years of Nero's reign was facilitated by the fact that Nero faced no major domestic or foreign problems that would have put him to the test. In the year 57, for example, Tacitus wrote that he had nothing particularly interesting to report, unless one were to count the construction of a new amphitheater.

Toward the end of the quinquennium, in 58, a motion was made in the Senate to award Nero the consulate for life, in order thus to tie him as tightly as possible to the

Figure 4   Portrait herm of Seneca (Berlin State Museums, Antiquities Collection, Inv. No. 391). Preußischer Kulturbesitz. Photo: Johannes Laurentius

Senate as an institution. Nero rejected the proposal, to the relief of a majority of the senators.

After the death of Burrus and Seneca's withdrawal from public life, Nero abandoned the restraint he had previously shown because he believed a course supporting the Senate promised to be less and less profitable. The first charges for high treason (*maiestas* trial) were brought in the year 62. This marked the beginning of the end of his concern for the Senate. At the end, in 67, when Greece was granted "freedom," Nero did not consider the Senate worthy even of being informed.

During his "accession to the throne" in 54, the expectations of the senatorial aristocracy were by no means unattainably high. No one expected Nero to present a "government program" in a modern sense, and all were perfectly content if only the known abuses of the Claudian

regime were avoided. As long as the emperor kept to tried
virtues such as *civilitas* and *liberalitas*, no one got the idea
to demand any far-reaching reforms and bold plans. All in
all, the relatively good initial years of Nero's reign stand
out all the more in comparison with the terror of his later
years. The participation of later victims of Nero in the
regimen of these early years made it seem necessary to the
senatorial reporters to explain their involvement by stress-
ing the modest advantages of the early years of Nero's reign.

IV

Matricide

Nero owed his taking the throne to his mother's intrigues, and the intensity of her influence made it inevitable that a crisis would come sooner or later. On top of that came the interests of Burrus and Seneca, whose gratitude to Agrippina for past favors was gradually replaced by their gratitude to the young ruler for more recent favors. Preliminary signs of the young ruler's independence were evident, and the first crisis in Agrippina's ambitious plans to have a share of the power came unexpectedly fast, hardly a year after Claudius' death. Among the instructive suggestions that Nero certainly had often to endure were Agrippina's comments about the fundamental political significance of his marriage to Claudius' daughter Octavia. At the time she was only thirteen years old and far more reserved than many other beautiful women at court. The marriage was obviously a purely dynastic formality.

Nero, however, fell madly in love with a young Greek freedwoman named Acte, who had also sought the attention of the young ruler. At first Nero succeeded in keeping the relationship secret from his mother, but then he had to listen to her reproach that he was neglecting his wife and thus jeopardizing the birth of a legitimate heir to the throne.

There is every reason to believe that Nero's feelings for Acte were sincere and, albeit less obvious, that Acte saw Nero not only as the ruler of the Roman Empire. Together with his two nurses she was to bury his remains in the year 68. Nero's intense relationship to Acte lasted at least three years. At times he had even thought of marriage, ignoring the political significance of his marriage to Octavia. There were consuls prepared to swear in the Senate to Acte's noble descent in order to eliminate the obstacles to marriage posed by her status as a freedwoman.

Agrippina sensed that Nero's advisors used his unanticipated serious relationship to Acte for them to win his trust by supporting it against the will and resistance of his mother. When harsh accusations proved useless, Agrippina tried to win back her former influence on her son through obligingness and kind words. She must have been incredibly bitter, having lost so much power in only a few months.

When Nero tried to appease her with a generous gift from the imperial wardrobe, her angry comment that it belonged to him through her efforts alone was an error that was difficult to undo. While that remark, which soon reached Nero's ears, might have been simply undiplomatic, her uncontrolled ranting about the advantages of Claudius' son Britannicus was alarming. Obviously notorious for her hurtful speeches, the "daughter of Germanicus," as she liked to call herself, also insulted the proud Burrus as a cripple and Seneca as an ambitious pedant. But these were errors that would be avenged.

Britannicus, whom Agrippina is said to have described as a worthy replacement for her son, died only a short time later. The son of Claudius was thirteen years old at the time. There were still forces at the court that kept an eye on the political future of the boy and he himself contributed to intensifying Nero's suspicion. At an extravagant *Saturnalia* festival, Nero asked him to recite a song in the vain expectation that the son of Claudius would embarrass himself as his father used to do at social appearances. But the opposite occurred. Young Britannicus was considered a good singer; he self-assuredly improvised a song about the fate of a prince who was robbed of his right to rule. If this scene can be viewed as a benchmark of Britannicus' astuteness – because he dared to sing about the injustice done to him – then the meditative Claudius left behind a promising son.

Ancient reports of the sudden death of the boy, brought on by a potion brewed by the experienced poisoner Locusta, are not immediately credible. Few poisons were known that took effect so quickly and reliably while at the same time could be discreetly given to the victim. Locusta, who later also trained students in her art, was perhaps truly a rare expert in her field.

Britannicus died during a banquet, that is, in public. The administering of poison in the presence of Nero would have been an act of cynical openness: No one whose career was important to him could have dared to accuse the princeps, who was present, of instigating such a deed. Claudius' son took a drink that was supposedly tested beforehand by a food tester but was served scorchingly hot and diluted with colder, poisoned water to make it drinkable. And so it was possible for death to result; on the other hand, the convulsions of Britannicus resembled those of an epileptic seizure. Nero observed the collapse of his young rival and commented on the cramps with a remark about earlier fits of epilepsy. The later emperor Titus, eldest son of Vespasian, witnessed the occurrence. Historical reports considered it beyond any doubt that Britannicus had been poisoned on orders of Nero. Suspicions of contemporaries were reinforced by the circumstances of Britannicus' unusually speedy funeral from which the public was barred. Those who were convinced of Nero's implication in the murder soothed their consciences with political considerations that the existence of a rival such as Britannicus would in the coming years have been a serious risk to carrying out ordered political business. And anyone familiar with the history of the time made excuses by referring to the fact that potential rivals had also died at the beginning of Tiberius' and Caligula's reigns. Malicious tongues claimed that after Britannicus' death Nero held Seneca and other advisors to him with generous gifts, which of course would have been difficult to refuse.

Agrippina, who was also present at the banquet, was hit hard by Britannicus' sudden death. Tacitus spoke of her utter horror and suggested to readers that she recognized that her son could be just as scrupulous as she. Before the year 54 she is said to have received a prophecy that her son would rule, but he would also kill his mother. "Let him kill her," she supposedly responded, "provided he is emperor" (Tac. *Ann.* 14.9). Perhaps she thought differently about that now.

From that point on she was intent on building up her own position of power to frighten her son, should he wish to become all too independent. After the death of Britannicus, Agrippina found an ally in the sad Octavia. She tried to win over the last remaining offspring of the Republican nobility and pulled together even greater wealth to use to gain political allies. Perhaps the strongest warning sign for Nero's advisors, she was also particularly affable in winning the sympathies of the praetorian officers of the bodyguard assigned to her as mother of the emperor.

Nero reacted very cleverly. A short time after Britannicus' death his mother was banished from the palace and forced to move into the nearby villa of her grandmother Antonia. On orders of her son not only her praetorian guard of honor was removed, but also the German troops. This was a clear signal to the public. The times in which the portrait of the emperor's mother appeared on coins were over, once and for all. Agrippina was pushed to the margins of political life. The number of visitors to the emperor's mother declined quickly; no one but her son himself continued to come regularly, as a demonstrative sign, only to leave all the faster after greeting her quickly and coldly.

Friendships came and went, but Agrippina did not lose the many embittered enemies that she had made over the past years. Junia Silana had several scores to settle: Members of her family were among Agrippina's victims. Consequently, it did not take more than an additional offense at Agrippina's biting remark about Silana's relationship to a far younger man for her to accuse Agrippina of treasonable activities against the princeps. Nero's Aunt Domitia, also a reliable enemy of Agrippina, saw to it that that charge was presented to Nero when a favorable opportunity arose – at a late hour when the wine already affected Nero's concentration and power of judgment.

The accusation made at that late hour was presumably totally invented, but it was well suited to convince Nero of the threat posed by his mother. She was allegedly planning to ally with Rubellius Plautus to overthrow the emperor. He was a direct descendant not of Augustus, but of Augustus' sister Octavia.

In crisis situations Nero always responded in panic, whether with or without wine. Trembling with fear, he wanted to have his mother and Rubellius Plautus executed without further investigation. Not only did Burrus owe his position to Agrippina; he was also well aware that it would be impossible to act against the "daughter of Germanicus," who was highly respected by the praetorians, without a trial and admission of guilt. He insisted that Agrippina first be interrogated. Nero's trust in Burrus was so lacking on the following day that he brought in Seneca and several freedmen when Burrus began his interrogation with a harsh tone.

Agrippina was able to defend herself against the charges with a presence of mind and the maliciousness that could be expected of her. There was evidently no indication whatsoever of any agreement with Rubellius Plautus. Her successful defense culminated in her receiving an audience with Nero. Agrippina's real or feigned anger was calmed through the promotion of some senators and knights that were close to her; and counsel for the prosecution were banished or condemned to death. The official explanation that important positions were filled by people of Agrippina's choosing made her appear almost as powerful as she had been in the past.

After the embarrassing incident regarding Silana's inconsequential charges, Nero must have eventually succeeded in pushing his mother more and more into political insig-

nificance, at least in comparison with the role she played
in the early part of his reign. He evidently felt safer from
her threats after 55. Personal encounters between them
became less and less frequent. When she came to Rome he
made sure her stay in the capital was unpleasant through
all kinds of legal disputes and, if a remark of Suetonius
can be believed, Nero had his mother harassed even at her
country residences.

Agrippina spent four years being forced into the background and had no choice but to accept all the humilia-
tion. Still, Nero decided to have his mother killed in March
59.

What drove him to such a command, which for contemporaries evoked horrific mythological scenes and memories of the decadent royal courts of the Hellenist period?
Nero's decision for matricide precisely in early 59 cannot
be easily understood from extant records.

What likely remained unchanged were the advice and
admonitions of his mother, expressed with her known intensity. It is actually surprising that Nero did not dare to
truly live out his artistic interests during his mother's life-
time; he waited for that until after her death. The degree of
his frustration with her is clearly expressed in Suetonius'
citation of the "threat" that he would abdicate and withdraw to private life on Rhodes (as Tiberius had done earlier
when he was dissatisfied with Augustus). If Suetonius'
passing remarks can be believed, then Nero had long been
so unnerved by the threatening advice and private sway of
his mother that he made three unsuccessful attempts to
poison her. These attempts failed because Agrippina had
anticipated such attacks through poison by having antidotes with her.

The difficulty that even contemporaries had in finding a
concrete reason for Nero's decision is obvious from Tacitus'
depiction. He explained both this and the previous crisis as
due to a woman's influence, just as in the year 55, when
Nero's love for Acte was presented as triggering the first
time he dissociated himself from his mother. In 59 it was

supposedly Poppaea Sabina, Nero's new love interest, who continued to torment the ruler about his dependence on his mother until Nero finally decided to kill her.

Poppaea was about six years older than Nero and not only attractive, but extremely ambitious as well. Based on typical criteria, only a resolute flatterer could refer to her background as noble. Her father, Titus Ollius, did not come from a senatorial family; and he died as a quaestor and follower of Sejanus in 31. The name Poppaea traces back, oddly, to her maternal grandfather Gaius Poppaeus Sabinus, who was a consul in the year 9 CE and long-time governor in Moesia, a province on the Danube. Her first marriage, which produced a son who was killed by Nero in 66, was to a praetorian prefect of Claudius, but the marriage did not last long. Her second husband was Salvius Otho, who was well liked by Nero. It was during her marriage to Otho that she began a relationship with the emperor. This love triangle was evidently the talk of the city for quite some time, until Nero transferred his friend and rival to the distant Lusitania (Portugal) in 58. There he proved himself as a governor, to the surprise of all who were familiar with his escapades in Rome's nightlife.

Agrippina would have spoken contemptuously of this lady with a past but no forebears. In contrast to Nero's relationship with the freedwoman Acte, the idea of legalizing this relationship (after a divorce) was not entirely unrealistic, and because Poppaea's fertility had already been confirmed through the birth of her son, there could be hopes of an heir.

Agrippina did everything in her power to prevent this change in her son's marital situation that was obviously in the offing. The scant information that has been passed down about Poppaea definitely makes that understandable. Not only was she experienced in producing exotic elixirs for a magnificent complexion, she evidently also had intellectual interests. There is every reason to believe that she was sympathetic toward the religion of the Jews. Flavius Josephus, the famous historian of the Jewish revolt against the Roman Empire, met her when he was an ambassador in 63 and he appreciated her support of Jewish affairs.

Later senatorial historians, who by no means stood out through valiant conduct vis-à-vis Nero, reported adverse details about Agrippina's attempts to tie Nero to her through an incestuous relationship that was nightmarish even by ancient standards. Those who were – in retrospect – especially ill-disposed toward Nero even pictured the son to have initiated the effort. All these threats to Nero existed only in the imaginations of later reporters. On the contrary, Nero kept as much distance from his mother as possible. The later encounter preceding her murder was a meeting following a long period of his having avoided all personal contact and was thus celebrated as a "reconciliation."

Despite the personal distance between mother and son, Nero was determined in spring 59 to get rid of Agrippina. Burrus and Seneca were told nothing of his plans. At first murder by poison was considered, but Nero determined that Agrippina, after having experienced Britannicus collapsing at the banquet, always had antidotes in anticipation of such an attack. It would have made sense to use praetorians for the deed, since they were accustomed to delivering death sentences. But although he had no explicit indications, Nero would have known that in this case the loyalty of his guard was not above all doubt. The only other option was the fleet soldiers at Misenum, whose commander Anicetus was one of Nero's teachers when he was a boy and – for unknown reasons – an enemy of Agrippina. He suggested to Nero that a ship be constructed with a cabin specially prepared so that at a suitable opportunity a beam would fall on the unassuming Agrippina, killing her.

Everything was prepared in Campania. At the five-day festival of Minerva in March 59, Nero invited his mother to a conciliatory visit, which supposedly pleased Agrippina in a motherly way. An event in her honor was held in the evening in a villa in Bauli. In contrast to the preceding years, Agrippina was given the seat of honor. Nero talked with his mother until it was night, in order to be able to carry out the attack prepared by Anicetus under cover of darkness. At a late hour Agrippina and two escorts were led onto the ship prepared in her honor.

Agrippina's lady-in-waiting Acerronia had just been talking about how well the evening had gone and the son's remorse over his mother's poor treatment when the signal was given to make the cabin collapse. One of Agrippina's escorts was struck dead. Acerronia and Agrippina, huddled together in the rubble of the cabin, noticed to their surprise that the ship was not supposed to be saved, but sunk. Acerronia, who had been seated at Agrippina's feet as a loyal friend, panicked and started shouting that she was the mother of the emperor. The cautiously silent Agrippina had to watch how Acerronia was beaten by the sailors in her stead. Only slightly injured on the shoulder, she swam toward shore and was picked up by a fishing boat that had noticed the shipwreck.

Agrippina had no further doubts about Nero's intentions to get rid of her inconspicuously, without a dagger or poison. But she thought it smarter for her to remain quiet. Her freedman Agerinus was ordered to inform Nero as quickly as possible about her fortunate rescue from the shipwreck. At the same time she said she needed some time to recover from the shock. Meanwhile, news spread that Agrippina survived the shipwreck. The residents made their way in the middle of the night to pay homage to the rescued Agrippina, evidence of her continued influence on the public even after all the years of being ostracized. All of this took place in the wee hours of the morning. The news of Agrippina having survived paralyzed Nero with terror. Again, he panicked. This time he was truly afraid of his mother. What would happen if she were able to mobilize the sailors and praetorians to her aid against Nero? If Tacitus correctly interpreted her cautious statements, however, Nero's fears were unfounded. In the hour of her greatest peril Agrippina was thinking not of a coup but of the testament of her wealthy companion, who had been killed by the sailors.

✦

As always when faced with difficult situations, Nero turned to Burrus and Seneca, whom he had wisely not told of his plans. Whatever was then discussed, the path that was taken to gain control of the situation was understandable. According to Tacitus, the two advisors remained initially silent in order to make Nero fully aware of the gravity of the situation. Burrus rejected the idea of getting the praetorian guards involved in the murder of the emperor's mother, which was now considered necessary. He said that the loyalty of the bodyguard toward all members of the imperial family would lead them to refuse to obey the order. Instead, Nero was told to turn to Anicetus, commander of the fleet. Luckily for the emperor, Anicetus, the old enemy of Agrippina, jumped at the chance. These decisions had hardly been made when Agerinus arrived with his message. Nero regained a grip on himself; he unscrupulously threw a sword at the feet of Agrippina's messenger and had him arrested as a detected would-be assassin. Were Burrus and Seneca, as his advisors, forced to witness this situation?

It did not take long for Anicetus' fleet soldiers to reach Agrippina's villa. They first drove away all the curious onlookers. Agrippina's servants were either arrested or had fled. When Anicetus finally approached Agrippina's dimly lit chamber, there was only one slave-girl with her, who also rose to leave. "Do you too forsake me?" Agrippina is said to have asked.

In the final moments of her life, Agrippina had extraordinary, if not to say imperial, composure. "If," said she, "you have come to see me, take back word that I have recovered, but if you are here to do a crime, I believe nothing about my son; he has not ordered his mother's murder" (Tac. *Ann.* 14.8).

Anicetus was with two men, who had orders to commit the murder. They uttered not a word, but merely swung their clubs. Agrippina's final words were spoken to the centurion who drew his sword to deal the deathblow. "Smite my womb" (*ventrem feri*, 14.8), she exclaimed, demanding that they strike the belly that gave birth to the matricide. This is a macabre gesture in many respects, full of allusions. At the moment of his death, Caesar paid attention not to appear in an unseemly manner as he fell. Agrippina on the other hand revealed herself entirely, violating all rules of female conduct and perhaps deliberately allowing the symbolic destruction of the site of female fertility on which the succession of the dynasty was founded.

Agrippina's body was quickly buried, like Britannicus', but without any demonstration of honor. More like a criminal, she initially was not even given a gravestone. Only later did a member of the household dare to put a very simple stone on the grave. Burrus knew what to do. He dispatched some praetorians to Nero to congratulate the ruler on being rescued from serious danger. Members of the royal household gave prayers of thanks in the temples.

Nero nevertheless had a hard time maintaining his composure. He did not yet dare to return to Rome, instead seeking refuge in Naples and from there sending a report on the death of his mother to the Senate. Everyone who listened astutely noticed from the announcement that it was not Nero who wrote the explanation, but Seneca. It took a particular kind of vanity to immortalize oneself in even that kind of statement.

According to Seneca, Agerinus was the assassin and Agrippina had taken her own life once the plans were revealed. Everything that she could have been accused of having done in the past was mentioned and even incredibly exaggerated.

Seneca had not been part of Nero's plans and for himself he may have thought his aid in dealing with the crisis was justified by the fact that there was no sensible alternative. Some people would have been pleased that Nero's position could not be threatened further by his unpredictable mother. The death of Britannicus had also been turned into an advantage in much the same way. The senators got carried away with extravagant decrees of gratitude and honor, but they did not give Nero any pleasure. He was tormented by nightmares and his guilty conscience never left him. Even on his later, extended travels to Greece, he avoided visiting Eleusis and Athens, which are otherwise part of the standard schedule of visitors to ancient Greece. It is very possible that he feared the Furies.

V

"What a loss for the Theater"

"Qualis artifex pereo," Nero is said to have wailed shortly before his death. "What a loss for the world of the theater." It is relatively certain that these words are authentic. They correspond to his identification as an artist, which increased in the final years of his life, especially as a kithara player, a specific meaning of the word *artifex*.

Nero's pleasure in appearing on stage contradicted all social standards of the Roman ruling class. He was reproached for this kind of "artistry" by the conspirators of the year 65. In the political pamphlets of 68, too, shortly before his fall, the accusations of being a "zither player" assumed a not insignificant role. The death of so many real or supposed rivals, the murder of Agrippina, and Octavia's cruel end presumably did not harm him any more than his irritating fixation on "art," since it was impossible to be both at the same time at that time in Rome: a princeps who lived up to the role expectations that had been binding since Augustus and at the same time a "marginal" artist – marginal according to the standards of his fellow aristocrats.

Broad cultural interests and the talent to express himself eloquently both verbally and in writing were part of the good form of the Roman elite. Nero's predecessors were no exceptions. Suetonius always mentioned the intellectual interests of the individual rulers in his biographies of the twelve Caesars. Julius Caesar's universal talents were at the very beginning of the Julio-Claudian dynasty. As an orator he was a match for any of his contemporaries and as the author of commentaries on his military campaigns in Gaul he was a first-class writer. Even dabbling in the art of poetry was permitted. Yet Caesar certainly had sufficient sense of quality to keep his manuscripts from the public eye.

Augustus also attempted to write poetry, but not without later criticizing himself and then burning manuscripts of dubious merit. The works he published himself were "political" writings such as his autobiography and, published posthumously, the *Res Gestae*, the résumé of his deeds, in which he struggled with every single word to find the right formulation. Augustus preferred to support the art of poetry as a patron.

Tiberius, the earnest successor, wrote verse not only in Latin, but also in Greek, parading his knowledge of the oddest details of Greek mythology in the style of an Alexandrian scholar. As far as is known, Caligula did not spend time on such matters, preferring to be noticed for his snobbish opinions of the classical poets Virgil and Livius. Even the critical Tacitus could not avoid commenting on Caligula's oratory talent. Nero's predecessor Claudius was a totally different kind of intellectual. In the decades prior to his being unexpectedly declared Caligula's successor, he tried to make a name for himself as a historian and antiquarian. As princeps he could look back on an extensive scholarly oeuvre, with works not only on Roman history but also on the history of the Etruscans and Carthaginians.

Nero's contemporaries kept mentioning the name Germanicus, Nero's maternal grandfather. He was said to have admirable competency in the Greek language and unusually broad literary knowledge. Germanicus' competent translation of Aratus' *Phainomena*, an astronomical poem of Hellenistic times that was overflowing with erudition, still exists today. In Greece Nero was also able to walk in the footsteps of his grandfather. Germanicus had even been to Alexandria in the year 19, a travel destination that

Nero never reached. Germanicus' interest in the antiquities of Egypt was so great that he traveled there despite Tiberius' express orders not to do so.

Nero's predilections went beyond the usual canon of aristocratic education from the very beginning, including not only poetry, but also music and sculpture. These were disciplines that had never before been considered worthy of a noble Roman. Young Nero encountered greater understanding from his first teachers, Beryllus and Anicetus, than from his mother. They were both later rewarded with high positions on the express wishes of the emperor. Beryllus was in charge of correspondence with the eastern realm of the empire and Anicetus became commander of the fleet at Misenum and, as previously mentioned, offered his services in the murder of Agrippina. Seneca was hired by Agrippina as a tutor in the year 50. His literary reputation gave special status to his tutoring task and at the same time made it clear what was expected of Nero. The fact that Seneca was told to keep the philosophy portion of his instruction to a minimum can practically be understood as a (later) accusation against Seneca for having taught a tyrant.

If Nero's determination in pursuing his interests can be seen as the norm, then a silent war was being waged between him and Agrippina from the very beginning. This did not at all correspond to the widespread notion of Agrippina's omnipotence over her adolescent son. At first the boy's willfulness was expressed in intense enthusiasm for famous charioteers. He was not allowed to talk about them and the tutors were ordered to curb Nero's passion. Anyone so inclined could see this as an unfavorable trait inherited from his father's side of the family. Even the grandfather, consul in the year 16 CE, was an ardent, and inglorious, charioteer, a leaning that was entirely inappropriate to his standing. Nero's interest in painting and sculpture, which was always mentioned along with music, was extremely unusual for a boy of his age and status.

What his mother had evidently been successful in preventing prior to his assuming the throne, Nero attempted to push through as princeps. Burrus and Seneca were also unable to do more than merely avoid the greatest embarrassment, thereby creating leeway for political decisions by the staff of advisors. The most famous kithara singer at the time, Terpnus, was called to the court at first to sing for the emperor day after day into the night and later also to instruct him. Menecrates, another "star" of the age, was also called in. From that time on, Nero worked untiringly on his training as a singer, rigorously trying to improve what was not a perfect singing voice. He left no effort by professional artists untried to prepare him for a veritable stage career. Wearing lead plates on his chest, he tried to strengthen his muscles. Supposedly detrimental foods were avoided, and laxatives were used to take care of the inner cleansing of the aspiring artist. Such efforts were explained by an unrestrained desire to perform in public and enjoy the earned applause.

Agrippina's opinion on all this was never in doubt, but as of the year 55 she had less and less of a say. Her rejection was understandable, since these leanings contradicted all rules for the Roman elite. Even if they enjoyed listening to professional musicians and even dabbled in the arts at times themselves, living out such musical interests was at best relegated strictly to the private sphere, and even there they were subjected to critical remarks. Calpurnius Piso, the leader of the conspiracy of 65 in name only, also had a talent for singing to the kithara. However, he was cautious enough to perform only in the smallest of private circles. This example shows that Nero's interest in performing was by no means an isolated case. Augustus had even passed legal requirements, to some extent in vain, to prevent the *jeunesse dorée* from engaging in activities inappropriate to their class, such as performing on stage and fighting as gladiators. While a blind eye could be turned regarding the "black sheep" of the great families, who were disinterested in a political career anyway, it took on a different dimension entirely when the princeps himself dared to question the rules. Nero's virtually exhibitionistic joy in performing must have threatened his reputation among the political elite; and it was capable of undermining his position in the long term. He was definitely aware of this fundamental violation of the rules. Not without reason did he later say that as princeps everything was permitted. Nero's artistry remained a private pleasure until Agrippina's death. His artistic interests must have taken up a lot of his time; painting and sculpture are mentioned although no further details are known.

Another of Nero's pleasures, though not without danger, was chariot races. Considerable training was necessary in order to control the teams of horses. In Greece Nero later learned how to drive a ten-horse team. Another time he fell out of the cart, though in his semiconscious state he was more worried about the correct placement of the victor's laurels than about his health.

Aside from music, Nero's interest in poetry was part of the more serious side of the "artist." His verses corresponded to the taste of the time, but they were probably far superior to the occasional epigrams of his imperial predecessors. Some turned out rather well, which could explain the widespread accusation that Nero loved to plagiarize. In 59 – after Agrippina's death – Tacitus wrote about Nero's guest dinners for talented but not yet famous poets. Nero listened attentively when they wanted to impress their host with new verses. This supposedly benefited his own verses, produced a short time later. As early as 51 Seneca referred to Nero's poetic abilities. Suetonius explicitly saved the honor of the poet; the biographer found manuscripts in the imperial archives with some of the more famous verses of Nero, which clearly show that he worked independently on his poetry.

The emperor had his poems and songs published with the characteristic title *Liber Dominicus* (The Master's Book), which Vitellius brought out in 69 to gain the favor of his guests. Only very few of the emperor's verses are extant; famous were, for example, a poem about the beautiful hair of Poppaea and an epos on Troy, from which some verses have been preserved. In contrast to most reports, here the hero was not the brave father Hector, but Paris.

The emperor-poet had great plans. Even before he started working on his Roman history epos, to rival Virgil and Lucan, he was advised on the recommended length of such a work. Flatterers suggested four hundred books, interesting evidence of the fawning courtiers that Burrus and Seneca were up against.

It is conceivable that contemporaries considered Agrippina's objections to Nero's artistic endeavors among the motives for the matricide, because directly after her death Nero dared for the first time to appear (semi)publicly as a kitharode (singing kithara player) and a charioteer. He made verbose efforts to justify this: The heroes of Homer and other ancients were charioteers, and singing to the kithara had already been ennobled because Apollo was the patron of the arts. Without Agrippina's support, Seneca and Burrus saw no alternative but to try to fulfill at least one of his wishes. It is typical that they favored chariot racing because of its masculine, military aspects.

Caligula had had a private racecourse beyond the Tiber. Though initially not open to the public, it was set up to give Nero an opportunity to race chariots. It was not long before spectators were admitted who showered the imperial racer with compliments. Soon other charioteers from the senatorial aristocracy were allowed to pursue their pleasure, to the amazement of Tacitus, who chose to explain their participation not through free will but through bribery.

In the same year, 59, Nero held the *Juvenalia* games in commemoration of the first shaving of his beard. What used to be celebrated in the circle of the family became a public event with performances in Greek and Latin. Men and women of rank appeared on stage. There was no uniformly high standard for the event; mockers made fun of consuls' performances and the dance formations of an eighty-year-old lady of irrepressible energy. And at the end of the festival the emperor himself took the stage. He carefully tuned the kithara and his singing teachers helped him find the starting note. Applause was certain: Starting with the *Juvenalia* in 59, a corps of young upper-class Romans called the Augustans led the applause in the style of the Alexandrian theater audience, in all acoustic variations, and they could be sure of making a speedy career.

Nero initiated a Greek-style festival in the year 60 that was to be held in a (Roman) five-year cycle. It was named the *Neronia* in honor of its creator. The musical portion of the several-day program, set up according to Greek tradition, included recitations and musical offerings; the athletic competitions were totally "non-Roman," in which the participants performed in the nude, reminding old-school observers of the – supposed – eastern vice of homosexuality.

Nero did not perform there in person, perhaps an indication that at the time he did still have the ability to consider the possible negative repercussions of an emperor appearing on stage. It is apparent that he attempted to grant legitimacy for the new festival by referring to the remotely comparable model of games (albeit celebrated only by Greeks) established by Augustus in commemoration of the victory at Actium. Nero received two first prizes. He gratefully accepted the first prize for Latin poetry and rhetoric. He declined the prize for best performance on the kithara, but instead had it placed at the foot of a statue of Augustus in an effort to demonstrate that the statue would in no way be dishonored by such a prize. The message was understood.

Historical tradition emphasized that Nero had an uncontrollable urge to perform in public. This easily overlooks the fact that Nero waited a long time after the festival games in the year 60 before his first totally public performance. Not until 64 did he perform as publicly as other artists did; even then, however, he performed not in Rome, but in Naples, which had a strong Hellenistic influence. Nero was thus fully aware of the risks he would have faced by performing in Rome.

His first audience was made up of his civilian and military entourage, curious residents from the surrounding

Figure 5 Nero as Apollo with a lyre. As (brass), ca 64–65 CE.
Hirmer Fotoarchiv

towns, and especially the enthusiastic populace of Naples.
Even a small earthquake that suddenly shook the theater
did not interrupt the performance. Nero was satisfied with
himself and his audience, who expressed their pleasure
in diverse modulations of applause. The dress rehearsal in
Naples was supposed to be followed by a trip to Greece for
additional performances, comparable to the trip to Greece
starting in 66. Nero was already on the road when for inexplicable reasons he decided to stay in Beneventum.

The first repetition of the *Neronia* games was scheduled
for the year 64, but the summer of the great fire was truly
the worst of times, so the repetition was postponed to 65.
Many senators feared Nero's wish to perform in person. At
the first *Neronia* they managed to satisfy the emperor by
awarding him all the first prizes. This time Nero asserted

his wish. If it was really about more than sheer exhibitionism, then perhaps he wanted to demonstrate his individual power to the Senate and gain popularity among the plebs of the city of Rome versus the Senate.

The staging of his first performance in Rome was carefully planned. He responded to the general call for a performance by the emperor with his "divine voice" by announcing he would sing in his gardens. A petition by the praetorians on duty who had joined the masses in wanting to see the emperor perform then convinced Nero to add his name to the list of performing artists. It was obvious that it was the emperor who had made his entrance on stage, and not any random artist, by the fact that he was escorted by both praetorian prefects, who carried the instruments, other praetorian officers, and the usual large entourage. Consular Cluvius Rufus offered to announce Nero's performance. Rufus remained respected even after Nero's death; he had a good reputation as a historian of the Neronian period and an author of a work on actors. He was certainly among those who considered Nero's performance to be less catastrophic than, for example, Tacitus later did.

Nero's pride in his talent was not totally uncalled for. The "fake" Neros who, after Nero's death, were popular in the east had to be rather good musicians in order to be believable. He gave great pains to have a rich and varied stage repertoire. Suetonius named some of his best roles, including not only relatively classical parts such as Antigone, but also exciting roles such as "Canace in labor" about the suicide of Canace after the incestuous relationship with her brother. There were also plays that made you think it would have looked better if Agrippina's murderer had not selected them: Orestes the Matricide and Blinded Oedipus. Nero's popularity among the people of the city of Rome ought to have increased through such imperial demonstrations of traditional taste, and he possibly thought at times of the political benefits of his "artistic" confrontation with the senatorial aristocracy. Conversely, his performances were increasingly used to control his political opponents. Whoever refused to make a sacrifice for the "divine voice" of the emperor, such as Thrasea Paetus, was immediately deemed an adversary. And whoever avoided the imperial performances or showed expressions of boredom or even dissatisfaction as a member of the audience, such as by falling asleep during the performance as the later emperor Vespasian did, risked being discovered by the emperor's informants – both undercover and in uniform – with all the resulting consequences.

It was occasionally presumed that Nero's philhellene initiatives and personal stage appearances served the edifying goal of making elements of Greek culture, which were not very esteemed, better known in Rome. This was hardly possible along the egocentric path Nero chose. In the end his art served, above all, repression.

VI

The Princeps and the Populace of Rome

Concern for the welfare of the common folk of the city of Rome was among the ruler's most important responsibilities. In Augustus' résumé of his deeds he attached great weight to the generosity he showed the *plebs urbana*. He was less concerned with philosophical charity for the needy than he was with guaranteeing peace and order in the capital. The last decades of the Republic had shown how much political pressure could be exercised by mobilizing discontented masses. Augustus therefore monopolized all donations and charity – ranging from grain shipments to cash gifts – for the ruling house and some loyal lieges. No other aristocrat should ever have the opportunity to draw personal advantage from the dissatisfaction of Rome's populace using the food supply or other current problems.

Even without a police force in a modern sense, the public order was maintained by the praetorian guard insofar as it concerned undesired expressions of opinions of individuals or smaller groups. Control of large assemblies of people in the theater or circus, which assured anonymity, on the other hand, was far more difficult and generally impossible without open use of force. Since Republic-style political assemblies no longer took place, the only remaining opportunity for someone to express their opinions relatively freely was in the theater or circus. Only here did the emperor encounter public opinion without being able immediately to defend himself. The mood in the theater could serve as a signal in difficult political situations. It was therefore very important that the expectations of the plebs regarding a well-regulated or even improved grain supply were met and, in addition, that critique of any kind was prevented among this segment of the population through all kinds of attractions.

The "anonymous" masses of the *plebs urbana* could largely be manipulated through far-reaching privileges, but this did not work all the time in every way. A false assessment of public opinion could lead to very detrimental consequences in a situation that was already difficult. One example of this from the time of Nero was the spontaneous enthusiastic outbursts over the (erroneous) news that Nero was reconciled with Octavia, who was loved by the people. Another example was complaints about the tax farmers that caused Nero to look into the situation. The goodwill of this segment of the "public" was always especially important when the princeps was experiencing difficulties with the political elite.

Beyond material favors, the populace also had other expectations that it would be a mistake for a ruler not to satisfy. "The people" loved it when those of higher status, including the princeps, did not make a point of rejecting their own pleasures. One of the greatest errors that Caesar made in the final months of his life was to sit in his circus loge initialing files instead of watching the bloody games. The expression of "public" displeasure was so great that Caesar changed his behavior. Augustus learned from this error, openly showing interest in the events taking place in the arena. From then on, visits to the theater and the circus became obligatory for all of Augustus' successors. The seating arrangement in the imperial loge also gave them an opportunity to keep abreast of the momentary power relations or to test the effects of a new personnel constellation.

Nero did not need to feign interest in the circus games and chariot races. He always felt drawn to such pleasures, even more so once it was considered proper for a young aristocrat. His enjoyment in personally participating in the more obscure comforts of the metropolis also far exceeded the norm. Of all members of the imperial household he seems to be the first to have made an effort to become better acquainted with the nightlife, under the cover of darkness disguised as a slave. At first he would move about on his own; later, after some dangerous brawls, he was protected by praetorians and gladiators in civilian dress. And so of all Augustus' successors, Nero was the one who best knew the depths of the city of Rome. His grandfather Germanicus had once mingled unbeknownst to the soldiers of his Rhine army in order to get to know the true mood among his troops. There is no indication, however, that Nero used his knowledge of some districts of Rome to learn more about the social hardship of the plebs.

He gladly satisfied expectations for generously financed celebrations, as Augustus had done before him. In order to underscore the traditional character of his *spectacula*, Nero had the equestrian order assigned to special seats, separate from the senators, thereby emphasizing the independent rank of the knights. Neronic extravagances at the games were no more sensational than what Claudius had offered. But while Claudius had a sadistic zeal and never tired of seeing gladiators die, Nero held fewer gladiator games than his predecessor. In this it is possible to recognize Nero's own initiative; if any "educational" impulse at all can be made out in Nero's actions, it was his desire to introduce games of Greek tradition to Rome.

Nero learned as a young man the political options that arose from dealing cleverly with the plebs. His first public appearance in the struggle for power that was choreographed by Agrippina was his participation in the Troy games, a traditional horsemen-battle game of the young aristocratic boys. The (totally spontaneous?) applause he received signaled to Claudius and his confidants that the aura of Germanicus was still important.

The declaration of Nero's coming of age in the year 51 was given special emphasis not only by an appearance before the Senate; on top of that, his position as heir to the throne was underscored by his gift of grain (*congiarium*) to the people. The circus games and animal fights after his marriage to Octavia in the year 53 also served to increase his popularity with the people of Rome.

To the end, Nero showed consistent concern for his popularity with the Roman populace, by no means only because of his obsession with applause, but in his awareness that it would be more difficult for him to do without this segment of public opinion than without the more critical segment of the senators. The poet Juvenal later mocked that "bread and games" represent the needs of the masses and a guarantee for the public order. Augustus had already recognized this, even without such discontented social criticism. Supervision of grain supply to the capital was occasionally centralized during the crisis years of the declining Republic, because the magistrates who would have otherwise been responsible would not have been able to handle the task. Augustus long avoided assuming personal authorization for the *annona*, the grain supply, as Pompeius held in the 50s, because he did not want to be accused of further expanding his power. Neither did he want to face the risk of failure, which he would then have had to bear alone. A number of supply crises in the decades of his reign led him ultimately to admit that this was a key issue for the capital and one best placed within the area of responsibility of the ruler. The first *praefectus annonae* was named in the final years of Augustus' rule. Augustus' successor had to pay careful attention that the grain ships arrived regularly. If any problems arose, things quickly became troubled in Rome. Claudius, for example, was once physically attacked by demonstrating plebeians during a food supply crisis, and his praetorian guard had difficulty saving him from greater injuries.

Nero, like his predecessors, let there be no doubt among the Roman public that he was responsible for the grain supply. In crisis situations he acted generously and parts of his significant building projects were aimed to further improve grain distribution. He intervened whenever special circumstances made it necessary for him to offset a price increase with his inexhaustible financial means or quickly replace supplies lost in transport. An interesting example of the clever stemming of a panic after three hundred grain ships were destroyed in the year 62 was his demonstrative destruction of large quantities of spoiled grain. Even then the prices did not rise – who would have doubted that the emperor had made provisions and could easily replace the three hundred shiploads. The emperor's concern about the urban grain supply was also used to explain why he interrupted his travels to Greece at short notice in 64.

Grain for the population of Rome, especially the roughly 200,000 official recipients of grain at no charge, came by freighter largely from Egypt and North Africa. Because Rome had no port of its own, most ships put into Ostia. The harbor was expanded under Claudius and a connection to the Tiber was created to facilitate further transport of the grain to Rome. Construction for these projects had already begun in 46, but they were finally completed during the reign of Nero. A picture of the new port on coins aimed to demonstrate to the public how much Nero did to satisfy his obligations.

A storm at sea in 62 showed that merely enlarging the port ultimately would not suffice to secure the transport route. Nero thus took up a major project of the Caesarian period to improve the food supply to the capital. Caesar had intended to link the port of Terracina, south of Ostia, with the Tiber through a canal. Nero went yet a step further. Presumably in the year 64, he started canal-building projects that were supposed to provide a connection between the port of Puteoli, where the grain freighters from Alexandria generally docked, and the Tiber. These projects were abandoned at the latest after Nero's fall, but the complaints of senators and knights cannot be viewed as a conclusive argument against the feasibility of the project. They felt their peaceful seclusion was being disturbed, and deplored the loss of quality of some vineyards in the area. Construction projects of this scale made it clear to the public in the

Figure 6 The port of Ostia: Lighthouse at the top; moorings at the left and right; ships at the center. The legend reads: Port(us) Ost(iensis) Augusti. Sesterce (brass), 64–68 CE. Hirmer Fotoarchiv

Roman capital even in the final years of Nero's reign that the emperor was not solely concerned with his art.

Nero's popularity among the social strata who must have been most interested in securing and expanding the system of grain supply remained intact into his final weeks. The "unrest" that was reported to Nero in Greece, and which provoked him to return ahead of schedule, can be explained not by his neglect of the *plebs urbana*, but by developments outside his control in North Africa, where the legate Clodius Macer had begun hatching plans of his own. Any supply problems that existed starting in the spring of 68 were due to the commencing obstruction of the North African grain route. In any case, Tacitus did not consider the food supply to have been among the factors that accelerated Nero's decline.

Not until the final weeks of his rule could Nero no longer reckon with the support of the people of Rome. At that time at least, the voices of public protest became louder than the approval that had been hitherto forthcoming. Attempts to levy troops in Rome itself failed miserably. Perhaps the emperor did not really perceive that any more; directly before his death he thought of giving a speech to the people of Rome.

The victor Galba entered Rome as an untimely strict old gentleman. It was not long before the memories of Nero's generosity and popularity were glorified. This belated popularity did not end with Galba. Instead, it remained intact for surprisingly long under the reigns of Otho and Vitellius in 69; that is why it had to be taken into consideration by both successors. Otho showed his respect for the deceased predecessor through his clothing and haircut. Some people said he also took on Nero's name in his title and had a large sum approved to finish the "Golden House." He thought such gestures and measures would strengthen his position in the capital. And Vitellius, who used to accompany Nero on his trips into the city's nightlife, did not think he could totally do without Nero's supporters. He held a burial ceremony for Nero on the Campus Martius. In a convivial circle he occasionally requested permission to recite plays from the *Liber Dominicus*, Nero's songbook. Once Vespasian assumed power such reminiscing became a thing of the past and it became advisable not to express all too lavish praise of the musical talents of his son Titus.

Nero was definitely successful in his efforts to gain popularity in the capital. The political significance of such popularity was indisputable, even among his predecessors. But it was a mistake to value the applause in the theater more highly than his reputation among the political and military elite.

VII

The Provinces of the Empire

Any Roman could have read in the *Res Gestae,* Augustus' résumé of his deeds, that a princeps was responsible for the welfare of the provinces and the expansion of the empire. The text was eternalized on bronze tablets on the mausoleum of the founder of the dynasty, as information also for the successors. Augustus was familiar with almost all provinces firsthand, as was Tiberius. Caligula wanted at least to undertake a campaign of sorts to Britain, and even Claudius, who was quite the opposite of a military man, had a British campaign organized in order to gain some military glory for himself. His son was named Britannicus after the triumph.

Nero, however, never left Italy until the year 66. This can be explained, for one thing, by his egocentric rejection of all of Rome's military traditions in favor of his artistic leanings and, for another, by his appraisal that the provinces could be controlled even without the presence of the princeps in person. Also, after Claudius' adventures in England, for a time there were no theaters of war so important or at risk as to require the emperor's presence. It was not until his late plans for a campaign in the Caucasus that Nero, too, no longer chose or could afford to ignore the military aspect of his public role as princeps.

Roman "foreign policy," at least in the early years, lay in the hands of Seneca, Burrus, and other experienced advisors. At first not only military issues were pushed to the background in hopes of peace at all the borders. Matters of provincial administration were in fact not taken up at all in the "policy statement." This is surprising because both Seneca and Burrus came from the provinces. A particularly Stoic, "caring" accent could have been expected, especially of Seneca. There is no indication that he showed any great interest in this part of his advisory responsibilities.

Administration of the provinces was generally better organized starting with Augustus than it had been during the time of the Republic. Big-time blackmailers such as Verres, famous through Cicero's charges, were a thing of the past. Of course there were always people attempting to feather their own nest, but the more covetous of the provincial administrators during the time of Augustus or Tiberius, for instance, were well aware that Republican-style excesses would not be tolerated.

In Neronian times there were a whole series of corruption trials that affected the welfare of the people in the provinces. Some of the guilty parties escaped conviction through intervention by the emperor because he had obligations to them. In Nero's defense it can be said that in many cases even the Senate itself was not all that interested in convicting incriminated members of their rank.

Provincial governors rarely became poorer during their period of office. And only very few philosophically inclined senators took seriously their responsibility to care for the population within their jurisdiction and withstood the ridicule of their fellow senators for such correctness. Anyone who strictly or demonstratively kept to the rules could be certain of attracting attention. The later emperor Otho, for example, conducted himself very differently in his province of Lusitania than his friends from Rome's nightlife would have expected.

Not everywhere in the empire did the troops stationed in the provinces remain in their field camps. The *Pax Romana* was an armed peace that was threatened in Neronian times at three locations: in Britain, Armenia, and, extending beyond the year 68, in Judaea.

Britain became part of the Roman sphere of influence under Caesar. His invasions of southern England in the years 55 and 54 BCE were merely a first small step in taking the island for the Roman Empire, even if Caesar himself worded it somewhat more confidently in his reports to the Senate. Augustus had limited himself to skillful diplomacy with the Roman-friendly kings of England, and Tiberius, too, dealt with more pressing issues than conquering the distant Britain. Caligula, who had previously lacked military merits, seriously considered planning an invasion of the island, which tempted him alone because of the crossing and "conquering" of the ocean that it would involve. For unknown reasons, though, he stopped at the channel coast.

Claudius, too, needed to show some proof of military prowess. The risky phase of the offensive was left to Aulus Plautius. According to imperial propaganda, Claudius in person came to the aid of his commanders, who were exhausted from the British resistance. After only sixteen days Claudius had decided the battle in favor of the Romans, and in the year 46 he celebrated the Roman Conquest over Britain, which was then made an imperial province. Reliable client kings were to ensure that any hopes of other tribes for independence would be restricted.

Nero's commanders were ordered to secure whatever they had attained and to take new territory only if opportunities were favorable. Didius Gallus, who had been appointed by Claudius, was content with the status quo, which despite the ridicule of contemporaries must have been difficult enough to maintain. His successor Quintus Veranius had resolved to conquer Wales. But Veranius died soon after and his successor Gaius Suetonius Paulinus was an ambitious military man imbued with a desire to match Corbulo, who had been so successful in the eastern provinces. The advance in Wales was stopped in 58 by news of a revolt of the Iceni (in the area of present-day Norfolk and Suffolk). King Prasutagus, who was well disposed toward Roman customs, had made Nero an heir in addition to his own daughters, in hopes of securing the Iceni position. Prasutagus' obligingness was poorly rewarded. The transformation of the region of the Iceni into a Roman province began with the king's widow Boudicca and their daughters suffering every conceivable act of despotism by the Romans on the ground. These excesses led quickly to a revolt by the Iceni and their allies. It is difficult to confirm reports that the revolt was triggered not only by the brutality of subordinate Roman soldiers and officials, but also by the exaggerated demands of Roman financiers who called for the untimely repayment of loans. Seneca was supposedly among them. Stoics were not prohibited from engaging in financial transactions, but the fact that Tacitus wrote nothing about the accusations, which were made with relish by the philosopher's enemies, speaks against Seneca's having had a culpable share in such dealings.

Suetonius encountered vehement resistance and on top of everything the rebels were led by a woman, the frighteningly forceful Boudicca. Roman officers might have been reminded of the old epics they had read in school when they saw the queen riding across the battlefield in her chariot. The rebels conquered Camulodunum (present-day Colchester), Londinium (London), and Verulamium (St Albans), with substantial casualties among the civilian Roman population. Many Roman businesspeople had to pay dearly for their quickly acquired prosperity. In 61 Suetonius managed to defeat Boudicca and her troops. The queen's battle had been in vain; as Cleopatra had done earlier, Boudicca poisoned herself to avoid being paraded by the Romans in their triumphal procession.

The following winter brought the Roman troops not peace, but constant readiness for battle. Suetonius was hard on his soldiers, no less so than Corbulo had been on the eastern frontier of the empire. The procurator Catus Decianus, whose mismanagement had contributed to triggering the rebellion, was replaced by someone who knew the west well: Gaius Julius Alpinus Classicianus belonged to the Romanized upper class of the Treveri. Nero personally intervened in answer to Classicianus' letters to Rome. Instead of sending a high-ranking senator, Nero sent the freedman Polyclitus to resolve the problems on the ground in 61, responding to what Tacitus considered false charges against Suetonius Paulinus.

With that, Nero opened himself up to the accusation, like Claudius before him, of allowing his freedmen too much power. Polyclitus must have been a capable man. To the indignation of Suetonius and traditional, "imperialistic" senatorial circles in Rome, he carried through the imperial directive that the time of military actions was past. On the other hand Suetonius was not immediately humbled; not until a year later when a tenable occasion arose was he replaced by Petronius Turpilianus, who had the task of securing peace. This was a man Nero could definitely count on; in 65 he would be decorated with the honors of a triumphator for the role he played in suppressing the Pisonian conspiracy.

The crisis over the Armenian kingdom, which was the focus of Roman policy in the eastern provinces from 53 to 64, persisted for years. Sources do not refer specifically to Nero's personal role in formulating the foundations of Rome's Armenia policies, but his active intervention in the British theater of war justifies assumptions that from the 60s on Nero did indeed have his own, albeit changing, opinions regarding fundamental issues of foreign policy. The diplomatic resolution of the situation in Armenia enabled him in 65 to present his policies, which did not focus exclusively on military decisions, in a grand way.

Armenia was situated between the Roman Empire and Parthia and, consequently, had strategic importance in structuring the relationship between the Romans and the Parthians. Augustus had not considered the Parthians dangerous enough to resume Caesar's war plans against them, which had become moot when Caesar was murdered. Contrary to all expectations of the Roman public, he decided in the end for a diplomatic regulation of Roman–Parthian relations.

Armenia was treated as a state that was dependent on Rome, but Augustus and his successors were not always able to install a king that was loyal to the empire. Such setbacks, of course, did not diminish the Roman aim to hold sway in Armenia. Toward the end of Claudius' reign, in 52, it came to an unexpected shift in power. A revolt at the court of the Armenian king led to a Parthian invasion that could not be warded off by the few Roman troops stationed there.

Shortly after Claudius' death, news reached Rome that Armenia had been taken by Tiridates, a brother of the Parthian king Vologaeses. This documented a preference given to Parthian interests in Armenia at the expense of the traditional Roman presence, which demanded a response from Rome. Among the obvious duties of the princeps was securing the frontiers of the empire and the Roman influence in the border states. In 55 the successful general Gnaeus Domitius Corbulo was given the task of reestablishing Roman influence in Armenia. Entrusting such a capable officer was publicly regarded as a sign of imperial self-confidence. Nero himself was probably not as personally involved in this decision as he was three years later regarding the dispatching of Polyclitus to Britain. Corbulo received a broad base of command and prepared his troops for a military campaign in Cappadocia. The troops were brought together from several provinces and even client princes were incorporated into the military plans.

After a long period of preparation, the attack was launched in 58. Corbulo's goal was not to eliminate Tiridates; in Nero's name he offered him a deal to retain his seat on the throne if he accepted Roman supremacy. The brother of the Parthian king refused, preferring to flee.

An appropriate substitute was sought in Rome. Did Nero participate in choosing the Roman candidate for the abandoned throne of Armenia? He was in any case personally acquainted with the person selected; Tigranes was the son of a former, unsuccessful Roman pretender and had lived in Rome. He was considered a willing tool of Roman interests.

A strong Roman contingent was assigned to secure his position and at the same time neighboring princes were given land bordering on Armenia in order to win them for the protection of the region.

Right after arriving in Armenia, however, Tigranes made the mistake of violating Parthian interests by attacking Adiabene, which the Parthians viewed as part of their kingdom. It is surprising that Roman advisors on the ground were not in a position to prevent Tigranes from embarking on this adventure. Vologaeses sent his brother, the cast-out Tiridates, to confront Tigranes and make a point of moving his own troops toward Syria in order to prevent Corbulo from advancing to Armenia.

One of Vologaeses' political foundations was to do everything possible to avoid open military conflict with the Romans. When Corbulo gave him the opportunity to avert the further advance of Roman troops and save face, he accepted the offer and sent delegates to Rome to negotiate the Armenian throne. All that is known about the course of the negotiations in early 62 in Rome is that the delegates returned without having achieved anything. It was at this time that Burrus died.

At the start of the crisis Corbulo is said to have received directives that were in line with his own diplomatic caution. But Lucius Caesennius Paetus, the new governor of Cappadocia and Galatia, spoke openly of the advantages of direct Roman rule in Armenia, thereby provoking an attack by the Parthians, who were obviously stronger. Corbulo sent troops to relieve him – to no avail. Caesennius Paetus had surrendered unexpectedly fast and made an agreement with the Parthian king that allowed the beaten Romans to escape Armenia. Vologaeses remained moderate and wanted to resume negotiations for Rome's recognition of his brother as king of Armenia.

Corbulo rejected all further actions to retake Armenia. This restraint corresponded to maxims of eastern policies tracing back to Augustus. Nero did not want to get involved in a direct military confrontation either; caution was advised on the basis of the geographical distance of such a war alone.

When in early 63 Vologaeses' delegation arrived in Rome offering that Tiridates would request Roman protection in return for official recognition, this shocked the princeps' advisors. The opinion at court had been made solely on the basis of the euphemistically positive letters of Caesennius Paetus. Now a centurion of the Syrian army, who had escorted the Parthians, gave the astonished gentlemen information about the true circumstances, the Roman defeat and the withdrawal from Armenia.

Nero consulted on this, not with his freedmen but in the circle of his senatorial advisors. It was possible to know in Rome that Vologaeses wanted to avoid a major confrontation with the Romans. For this reason, the decision for a mass mobilization in the war region was considered a good means by which to emphasize Roman interests. Vologaeses continued to seek a diplomatic solution; a compromise that was tenable for both sides seemed to be the same thing that had been offered earlier: Tiridates would be willing to lay down his royal headband, the diadem, at the foot of a statue of Nero and solemnly declare that he would not wear his crown again until he received it from the hands of Nero in Rome. That was an unusual gesture of humility for the Parthian Tiridates. His future Armenian subjects, on the other hand, were used to their rulers being dependent on the favor of Rome.

This agreement was made in 63, but Tiridates took his time getting to Rome. First he went to his brother, the Parthian king, to prepare his journey and negotiate further conditions. One of his daughters remained with Corbulo as a hostage. Nero also used the time up to Tiridates' arrival to try to gain public support. It was important to convey the outcome of the long battle as a military victory to the Roman public. The end of the fighting was celebrated with the ceremonial closing of the gates of the Janus Temple as a sign of peace throughout the empire under Roman supremacy. No one wanted to speak of the fact that Rome's position in the east had actually been weakened.

Tiridates spent nine months traveling from Armenia to Italy, where he arrived in the summer of 66. The journey is said to have cost 800,000 sesterces each day, equivalent to almost the value of a senator's property qualification at the time. Wherever the entourage arrived local dignitaries had to demonstrate their generosity, so the trip was a financial burden for all provinces Tiridates passed through. He was escorted by Parthian nobles as well as Romans, including Annius Vinicianus, a son-in-law of Corbulo. It had been agreed that Tiridates would not have to visit the provincial governors and that he would be treated like a senator of consular rank. The journey was slowed down due to the fact that he was a Mithraist and refused to travel by sea, except for crossing the Hellespont (Dardanelles). He made the entire trip on horseback. At his side was his wife, also on horseback; she protected her face from intrusive looks with a helmet instead of the usual veil. The travel route in Italy itself was set by Nero. After arriving in northern Italy Tiridates, who had been given a chariot drawn by two horses for the journey, was not brought directly to Rome; instead he received instructions to meet Nero in Naples, the emperor's favorite city.

As he had been ordered, Tiridates paid homage there to his Roman sovereign, except that he did not permit his dagger to be removed even during his meeting with Nero. He allowed only that it be nailed to the sheath to render it unusable. From Naples, Nero and Tiridates then traveled to Rome via Puteoli, where Patrobius, one of the emperor's freedmen who had come to wealth, organized elaborate gladiator games. It is reported that Tiridates proved his skills there as an archer. With a single arrow he supposedly killed two bulls, which must have excited the spectators, who loved such excesses.

The main ceremony at the Roman Forum had been planned down to the last detail. Spectators had already taken their seats the night before; soldiers and civilians were separated. At daybreak Nero appeared in the traditional dress of a Roman triumphator, escorted by senators and praetorian guards. As soon as Nero had taken his seat on the rostrum, Tiridates made his way with his entourage past the praetorian honor guard and paid homage to Nero as if the emperor had been an incarnation of the god Mithras: "Master, I am the descendant of Arsaces, brother of the kings Vologaesus and Pacorus, and thy slave. And I have come to thee, my god, to worship thee as I do Mithras. The destiny thou spinnest for me shall be mine; for thou art my Fortune and my Fate." (2) The princeps answered majestically, "Well hast thou done to come hither in person, that meeting me face to face thou mightest enjoy my grace. For what neither thy father left thee nor thy brothers gave and preserved for thee, this do I grant thee. King of Armenia I now declare thee, that both thou and they may understand that I have power to take away kingdoms and to bestow them." (3) (Cassius Dio 63.5 (2, 3))

This performance was regarded as one of the highlights of the Neronian period, even by otherwise skeptical reporters. Another programmatic demonstration was when Nero was proclaimed imperator, a victorious commander, for the eleventh time. The diplomatic resolution of the Armenian conflict was thus judged a victory on the battlefield. The last stage of this military form of a diplomatic solution was Nero's resolution to give himself the name imperator as the highest sign of his identification with Roman tradition.

Tiridates returned home laden with gifts; the return journey went faster this time without any fear of traveling by sea. A generous delegation of Roman artisans was commissioned to rebuild the city when it was announced that the name of Artaxata, the capital which had been destroyed by the Romans, would be changed to "Neronia." Tiridates was able to rule Armenia without risk until the Alans invaded in 72; it seemed as if a region along the eastern border of the empire that had been endangered for years had finally been secured. The compromise with the Parthians guaranteed stability. The public response to the homage celebration of the new Armenian king in the summer of 66 reinforced Nero's feeling of certainty that he could leave Rome and Italy for an extended period of time.

A modern observer might view this as a clever way of exploiting a situation that was by no means advantageous for Rome. But it was not received in the eastern realm of the empire as an indication of Nero's weakness, which could be taken advantage of either politically or militarily. After the ceremony in 66 Nero enjoyed undisputed popularity in the east, not least among the Parthians themselves. Nero was aware of this; in fact, in the final days of his rule he could even think of the Parthians as a final refuge to escape his pursuers.

Nero had experienced only the very beginning of the dangerous developments in another part of the eastern border, in Judaea. His appointment of Vespasian as commander in the war against the Jews would have repercussions that no one could have foreseen at the time. When Nero sent Vespasian from Greece to Judaea, he had chosen an experienced military officer. He did not need to fear any far-reaching political ambitions because of Vespasian's knightly background, unlike the case of Corbulo. Even shortly before his appointment, Vespasian is reported to have incurred Nero's extreme displeasure when he was overcome by sleep during a performance by the emperor.

While the destruction of the Temple in the year 71 was an epochal break in the later history of the Jews, Roman observers at first did not see it as particularly threatening. After an extended period of mismanagement by the descendants of Herod, the land of the Jews had been declared a Roman province by Augustus in the year 6 CE. It was administered by a governor of knightly descent – at first called a prefect and later procurator – and a small number of auxiliary troops. The famous Pontius Pilate had not made any major career jump when he was transferred to Judaea. The establishment of a prefecture indicates how Judaea was initially assessed in Rome. Sardinia, Corsica, and the less settled parts of the Iberian peninsula were also prefectures at the time; they were difficult areas for the civilian administration but without any major significance. Although it soon became clear that the administration of Judaea was anything but easy, those in charge in Rome were not very lucky in their selection of procurators. Claudius had sent Tiberius Julius Alexander of Alexandria, who had broken with the Jewish faith, and thus his choice must not have pleased the pious Jews. And Gessius Florus, who was appointed in 64, was sent to Judaea not for any particular specialized knowledge, but because of his wife's good relations to Nero's wife Poppaea. Florus was actually totally unsuited for the position; he was of Greek descent and made no secret of his sympathies for the Greeks residing in Judaea. The revolt that ensued was ultimately triggered by Florus' corrupt behavior in the dispute between Greeks and Jews over influence in Caesarea and the confiscation of outstanding tax payments from the Temple treasury. The first acts of violence came in the early summer of 66, right around the time when Tiridates was received in Rome. A short time later a segment of the priesthood in Jerusalem pushed through the decision to no longer perform the traditional sacrifice on behalf of the emperor. When in the course of the inner-Jewish conflict over this decision auxiliary Roman troops were murdered, war became inevitable. Syrian governor Cestius Gallus was not able to handle the situation and experienced severe defeats in the course of 66. This forced Nero to take action.

In spring 67 at the latest, Vespasian was appointed in Greece after having had to wait many years for an adequate command position. Now he became part of Nero's entourage and was exposed to harassment by the courtiers. Vespasian achieved brilliant military victories in the initial months of his command. Jewish prisoners of war were sent to Corinth, where they were put to work building the isthmus canal.

Nero never could have imagined that the future victor over the Jews would develop far greater ambitions. It was inconceivable at the time for him to have been a rival for power. Only later authors depict a Nero who was plagued by fearful nightmares about his successor Vespasian – literary revenge for Vespasian's fear of Nero and his fawning courtiers in Greece.

VIII

The Great Fire of Rome

After the death of his daughter Claudia Augusta in 63, only a few months after her birth, Nero sought solace in yet greater extravagance and daring plans. He took more liberties on the stage in Naples in early 64 than ever before. For the first time he performed not in his own gardens, as in Rome, but blatantly in public. Naples was Nero's favorite city because of its Greek influence. In spite of all his activities, Nero never forgot to insure his security. He ordered Torquatus Silanus to commit suicide since Silanus was a distant relative of Augustus, and thus a potential rival, and he had a compromising predilection to give his house personnel official titles like the freedmen at the imperial court.

Nero's performance in Naples was something like a dress rehearsal for greater events. As mentioned above, Nero planned a trip to Greece but it was postponed at the last minute. Then he planned to visit the eastern provinces and Alexandria. Constructors in Egypt were commissioned to build a bathhouse for the high-ranking visitor. The last member of the imperial household that had traveled there was Nero's grandfather Germanicus, who had fostered and enjoyed his popularity, much to the dismay of the strict Tiberius.

Nero countered concerns about his plans for an extended absence with a calming edict to the people of Rome. He would not be gone long, he said, and everything was taken care of. But this trip did not happen either, the official reasons being unfavorable times or simply Nero's awareness that he could not feel certain about Rome. An edict pronounced that the emperor refrained from his personal desires in order to spare the citizens the worries that his absence might bring. The temporary interruption of all plans was marked by celebrations designed to show the people of Rome how pleasant the care of the princeps was for those wishing to be entertained. In view of the very permissive nature of some of the merrymaking, more morally strict senators let it be known that Nero and his royal household would be better endured the farther away their future travels would take them. The odd wedding celebration of the princeps with the handsome former slave Pythagoras gave the festivities an especially orgiastic accent.

The excessive life at the court came to a sudden end by the great fire that broke out on the night of July 18 and destroyed vast segments of the capital. There had repeatedly been larger fires in the city; the last had burned during the reign of Tiberius. The closeness of the buildings and the carelessness of the residents facilitated such fires. Augustus was the first to organize a regular fire department (the *vigiles*), but this precaution was never sufficient to really keep major fires in check.

The fire started in the Circus Maximus and spread to neighboring shops and stalls made of highly inflammable materials. Winds did the rest and soon the blaze was out of control. Of the fourteen urban districts that Augustus had built, only four were spared. Three districts were considered totally destroyed. Rome burned for six consecutive days, and after the flames had been initially extinguished, the fire then flared up again for another three days.

By establishing a fire department Augustus had set a signal that matters of safety were among the obligations of the ruler. He and his wife Livia were themselves present at fires in order to encourage the helpers. As a widow Livia continued the practice, to the horror of her son Tiberius. Claudius once spent two days and nights nearby a fire that was difficult to extinguish, offering assistance in the form of money and words of support.

Of course the populace in the year 64 expected the same; and Nero did not meet such expectations at all, or else only delayed. At the time the fire broke out, Nero was in Antium, about forty miles from Rome. He did not return immediately, but only when the flames started to threaten his palace, the *Domus Transitoria*. Later reporters might have exaggerated the delay in his arrival. Once in Rome, however, he did actively help those who were either threatened by the fire or already homeless. His gardens were made available to the needy and temporary shelters were hastily erected. Foodstuffs at reduced prices were brought to Rome from Ostia and other nearby cities.

His late arrival in Rome brought the public rage down on Nero. Some who had just heard about the emperor's performances in Naples must have believed that Nero was capable of deliberately setting the fire to support his own construction plans. One rumor led to another and eventually people were certain they had seen shadowy figures committing arson. The victims of the fire disaster were soon convinced that the emperor himself and his accomplices, especially the adverse Tigillinus, had caused the catastrophe. Was it not quite in the style of an emperor ready for the stage that he would sing – as was heard in whispers – about the burning of Troy from a tower or the roof of his palace, with the flames of the capital as a realistic backdrop?

Tacitus did not vouch for the accuracy of this rumor. The "Pisonian Conspiracy" of 65 was in the offing at that time. The courageous praetorian officer who maligned Nero as an arsonist shortly before his execution may have considered Nero capable of singing the arias about the fall of Troy.

The public anger went virtually out of control when it became known that the source of the secondary blaze could be localized in a garden of Tigellinus, of all places. People believed the praetorian prefect was capable of any scandalous

deed, including arson to promote the emperor's construction plans. All gifts, bribes, and vows were fruitless; the
rumor that Nero and his henchman were responsible for
the destruction would not go away.

Knowledgeable advisors, perhaps Tigellinus himself,
named a religious group from among the Jews that could
be scapegoated and made the target of people's rage. Tacitus
was the first pagan author who mentioned Christ and the
Christians in this context:

But all human efforts, all the lavish gifts of the emperor, and the
propitiations of the gods, did not banish the sinister belief that
the conflagration was the result of an order. Consequently, to get
rid of the report, Nero fastened the guilt and inflicted the most
exquisite tortures on a class hated for their abominations, called
Christians by the populace. Christus, from whom the name had
its origin, suffered the extreme penalty during the reign of Tiberius
at the hands of one of our procurators, Pontius Pilatus, and a
most mischievous superstition, thus checked for the moment,
again broke out not only in Judaea, the first source of the evil,
but even in Rome, where all things hideous and shameful from
every part of the world find their centre and become popular.
Accordingly, an arrest was first made of all who pleaded guilty;
then, upon their information, an immense multitude was convicted, not so much of the crime of firing the city, as of hatred
against mankind. Mockery of every sort was added to their deaths.
Covered with the skins of beasts, they were torn by dogs and
perished, or were nailed to crosses, or were doomed to the flames
and burnt, to serve as a nightly illumination, when daylight had
expired. Nero offered his gardens for the spectacle, and was exhibiting a show in the circus, while he mingled with the people
in the dress of a charioteer or stood aloft on a car. Hence, even for
criminals who deserved extreme and exemplary punishment, there
arose a feeling of compassion; for it was not, as it seemed, for the
public good, but to glut one man's cruelty, that they were being
destroyed. (Tac. *Ann.* 15.44)

Although Nero was not regarded as a persecutor of Christians until much later reports by Christian authors, there
is no good reason to doubt Tacitus' report. Most observers

at that time regarded the Christians as a Jewish sect that behaved by and large like the Jews of Rome, who had enjoyed special status since the times of Caesar. They were given the privilege of being allowed to practice their religious obligations even if this meant not complying with the usual practice of honoring the ruler. Nero's advisors could have just as easily pointed to the Jews of Rome as the arsonists, since they were repeatedly accused of failing to honor the emperor and participate in everyday life as familiar to the Greeks and Romans. Such detachment was criticized as "hatred against mankind."

Only two years were to pass before the revolt broke out in Judaea. There are indications that some men and women in the sophisticated circles of the emperor's court sympathized with Judaism. This could be why not the Jews but the Jewish "splinter group" that followed Christ was made into a scapegoat. Over the years the Christian community continued to grow through the efforts of Paul and Peter.

Nero had chosen his scapegoat well. Christians were so unpopular among the upper classes that Suetonius came to the conclusion, based on his readings on the great fire of Rome, that at the time the emperor had acted in the interest of public security by containing a sect that was dangerous to the public. Nero could assume that the people of Rome would have a similar dislike of Christians, and he could thus purge himself of any suspicion. Tacitus' reference to sympathy felt by the public in view of the cruelty of the numerous executions is surprising. This concerns the victims, on the one hand, and of course criticism of Nero's cruelty, on the other. Were the people of Rome shocked at the large number of executions or where they moved by the brave behavior of the victims, including Peter and Paul, as was later presumed? The atrocious idea of wrapping those condemned to death in garments soaked in pitch to make them into living torches seems to have been a personal contribution of Tigellinus that later served as an example of the excesses of Nero's henchmen. It is hard to understand why early Christian authors did not mention the suffering of Christians in the year 64. Tertullian, who wrote at the end of the second century, was the first to refer to Nero as a persecutor of Christians because of their religious beliefs.

The members of the group that was given blame for the burning of Rome and sentenced to such particularly cruel deaths were not convicted because of their profession of a new faith, however, but for the alleged arson. The death penalty described by Tacitus corresponds to the usual penalty suffered by people found guilty of arson.

Anyone who despite the confessions tortured out of the Christians still believed that Nero had an interest in burning down the city could make reference to the buildings that the princeps had constructed after the fire. Nero did not break any traditions of the dynasty by building a lot and with pleasure; quite the contrary: even Augustus, in the résumé of his deeds, had boasted of his building projects in Rome. The erection of useful constructions and magnificent temples by the ruler or his friends was considered welfare for the common good. Augustus did in fact totally change the urban features of Rome, and he was proud of it. Suetonius cited Augustus as having said that he had found Rome as a city of brick and left it as a city of marble. Augustus had passed down to his successors the obligation to continue beautifying Rome. False thriftiness would lead to an unfavorable contrast to the founder of the dynasty. The reserved Tiberius, too, did not allow any doubt regarding this tradition and even some of Caligula's building projects were generally respected. Claudius also initiated some major construction projects, such as water pipelines in the capital, and several large endeavors that aimed to improve food distribution in Rome.

High construction costs for water lines, temples, and city walls were considered legitimate in the public eye; it was more difficult for rulers to gather public support for purely personal luxury constructions. The populace was used to the aristocracy's extravagant architectural projects from the final decades of the Republic and no one resented Augustus or any of his successors if their residences corresponded to the prestige of a world power. The demands of the upper class were high and continued to grow. If they showed restraint around the capital for reasons of discretion, they allowed themselves all the more luxury in Campania. The more magnificent villas in Pompeii and the murals on their walls with extensive residential landscapes can convey an impression of the expensive taste of the times.

Even before the fire, Nero had completed the construction of useful structures that had been started in the Claudian period and he also commissioned his own projects. Among those completed before Rome burned was the port of Ostia, a large marketplace (*Macellum Magnum*), an amphitheater at the Campus Martius, and, the pièce de résistance, luxurious thermal baths that later continued to bring praise from Nero's worst enemies. These and other structures that were restored after the fire appeared on coins to draw public attention to these examples of how the ruler satisfied his obligations.

After the fire in 64, the need for many new constructions and repairs in the devastated districts of the city was prudently taken advantage of to pass new security measures in order to avoid similar disastrous fires in the future. Some of these measures had existed since Augustus but had never been enforced. Older people grumbled about the less cozy, widened streets and the strictly controlled restricted maximum height for new buildings, which they felt increased the risk of scorching from the sun. In fact, however, Nero and his urban development advisors earned much-deserved praise regarding the future safety of the city. The emperor made ships available at no charge to transport the incredible masses of construction rubble down the Tiber to Ostia. Nero personally financed only a small portion of the many building measures that were necessary; specifically mentioned were the innovative porches that he paid for, which were supposed to slow the flames down from spreading to the main buildings. Anyone who financed the reconstruction of private residences was awarded attractive privileges, including even the granting of full civil rights for those whose rights had previously been restricted.

Nero's violent end can perhaps explain why the thoroughly traditional and beneficial aspects of many of his building projects are devalued or not mentioned at all. Instead he is traditionally remembered only for a single construction project, which is emphasized as proof of the megalomania of his building policies: the "Golden House" (Domus Aurea). Construction of this palace complex in the center of Rome was started after the fire and had not yet been completed in 68.

Nero took advantage of the destruction in Rome's city center between the hills of Palatine and Esquiline to build an expansive and architecturally very innovative estate. It cannot be surprising that some of the emperor's opponents drew connections between his project – which included many plots of land that had already been developed for housing and other uses – and the fire itself, which freed up the land for the future construction site.

Before the fire, Nero lived in the so-called "Domus Transitoria," an extension of the palace in which Tiberius and Caligula had resided, with a connection to the imperial gardens on the Esquiline. This building was in keeping with conventional rules of imperious living. The "Domus Transitoria" was destroyed in the fire. Nero grabbed the chance to conceive a totally new, unusually spacious design. Severus and Celer, the architects assigned to the project – who are otherwise unknown in the sources – had a reputation for daredevil and extravagant designs at the limits of what was technically possible.

Suetonius described the "Golden House" in a section on the extravagance of the emperor as follows:

There was nothing however in which he was more ruinously prodigal than in building. He made a palace extending all the way from the Palatine to the Esquiline, which at first he called the House of Passage, but when it was burned shortly after its completion and rebuilt, the Golden House. Its size and splendor will be sufficiently indicated by the following details. Its vestibule was large enough to contain a colossal statue of the emperor a hundred and twenty feet high; and it was so extensive that it had a triple colonnade a mile long. There was a pond too, like a sea, surrounded with buildings to represent cities, besides tracts of country, varied by tilled fields, vineyards, pastures and woods, with great numbers of wild and domestic animals. In the rest of the house all parts were overlaid with gold and adorned with gems and mother-of-pearl. There were dining-rooms with fretted ceils of ivory, whose panels could turn and shower down flowers and were fitted with pipes for sprinkling the guests with perfumes. The main banquet hall was circular and constantly revolved day and night, like the heavens. He had baths supplied with sea water and sulfur water. When the edifice was finished in this style and he dedicated it, he deigned to say nothing more in the way of approval than that he was at last beginning to be housed like a human being. (Suetonius, Nero 31:1–2)

The construction was still not totally completed when Nero died. Otho, who was in power for several months and definitely an admirer of Nero's taste, tried to continue the project. But after him no one was interested in finishing the controversial palace. Vitellius, who succeeded Otho in 69, did not like the "Domus Aurea" and his wife liked it even less. When Vespasian came to Rome victoriously in 71, the "Golden House" and the entire plot of land was given a provocatively different use. What seemed more reasonable than to make the imperial property truly public by building the Colosseum, the largest amphitheater Rome had ever seen? It was at the site where Nero, who did not like the bloody gladiator games, had had a beautiful pond laid out.

The wings of the "Domus Aurea" that had been completed by 68 were either torn down by successors or integrated beyond recognition into their own buildings. If Nero had lived longer – he was only 27 years old when construction commenced in 64 – and if his architects had had more time, he might have been remembered as one of the greatest builders in Roman history.

Figure 7   Vaulted hall of the *"Domus Aurea."* © 1990, Photo
Scala, Florence – courtesy of the Ministero Beni e Att. Culturali

The relatively little that can be clearly identified as part
of the original *"Domus Aurea"* is enough to demonstrate
that the architects and artists involved in the project were
masters of their trade. The vaulted structure of the octa-
gonal room at the center, for instance, was something totally
new, having no known precursor in Roman architecture.
No less innovative than the building technology was the
interior decorating, a creation of the painter Famulus, who
designed the walls with patterns and colors that were
unheard-of even in the boldest villas of Pompeii. A "true"
Roman and aware of his significance, he painted in a toga
instead of a smock. The first discovery of such frescoes in
the cellars (or caves, "grottoes") underneath the later baths
of Trajan in the late fifteenth century led to the coining of
the term "grotesque"; the interior design provided much
inspiration for artists of the Renaissance.

What in retrospect is a daring architectural design of the
avant-garde, which could have given Nero's presence in

Rome a very different character, was dismissed by contemporaries simply as an example of the emperor's excessiveness. On closer look, however, it becomes apparent that it was not the unusual design splendor of the new palace that incurred such displeasure. Precious metals, ivory, and jewels were familiar materials for the construction of luxury villas, and rulers were to some extent considered entitled to them. What annoyed all classes of the Roman populace was not the décor of the new building, but the unheard-of expansiveness of the entire grounds, which incorporated a part of the city center that had previously – before the fire – been open to public use. Nero's palace was not simply a palace, albeit huge, in the usual sense. It was an imperial palace and garden complex whose design, according to contemporary standards, belonged far outside the city gates. The villa complex in Tibur that Hadrian later used offers a comparison. To better understand the contemporaries it is necessary to know the precise land area covered by the grounds of the "Domus Aurea." By far the most cautious estimate is about the size of today's Vatican City, over one hundred acres.

IX

Opposition

Nero had experienced at the court of Claudius how inse-
cure the position of a princeps was, all displays of honor
and flattery notwithstanding. Discontent with how authority was exercised combined with personal ambitions of
critics could become life-threatening for the incumbent. It
was not senatorial moralists who posed the greatest threat
in his initial years in power. Nero had won over that group
with his inaugural speech, edited by Seneca. He could
initially count on the Senate's satisfaction with the new
regime, as well as the loyalty of the praetorians under the
leadership of Burrus. In fact, it was not all that hard to win
the sympathies of the people, provided the princeps promised to do everything better than Claudius had done.

A more real danger was presented by men whose relationship to the founding father of the dynasty was no more
distant than Nero's, since the only rule of succession at
that time was that an heir had to be related to Augustus.
Augustus' family and marriage policies had led over the
years to a number of such (desired and undesired) potential
heirs to the throne.

Not a single one of these last blood relations of Augustus
outlived Nero. Apart from Britannicus, who already suffered
the fate of an interfering pretender to the throne in 52, and
Agrippina, whose angry sense of vengeance was perceived
by Nero more and more to be a threat, these relatives were
thought to jeopardize the security of the princeps on account

of their equally ranked relationship to Augustus alone. Marcus Junius Silanus (consul in 46), whose unshakeable composure, reinforced by his wealth, inspired Caligula to give him the nickname "the golden sheep," was killed as early as 51 on orders of Agrippina. Rubellius Plautus was the last remaining rival whose relationship to Augustus could be explicitly referred to as on a par with Nero's. He was exiled to his estates in Asia Minor in 60 and then killed in 62. In 64, Decimus Junius Silanus Torquatus, brother of the victim of 51 and, like Nero, a great-great-grandson of Augustus, had to die. There were no remaining male descendants of Augustus, and in fact there were no young women, such as Nero's wife Octavia, whose high position could easily have inflamed the love of an ambitious young nobleman.

The emperor's praetorian bodyguard had sworn an oath on the entire imperial family. Only the "*Domus Augusta*" could be expected to satisfy the guard's hopes for reward. Even the most spirited of senators would have been a poor man within days if he aimed to fulfill their requirements.

A princeps could therefore do just about anything he wanted without risking the loyalty of his praetorians. Nero's artistic escapades were an example, such as in his final years, 65 or later, when he was put in chains on the stage for the "Frenzy of Hercules," and a praetorian jumped to his aid. Such naïve loyalty could not always be expected of the officers of the praetorian guard. It was a sign of Caligula's arrogance when he teased the high voice of one of his officers and then gave his mocking words yet greater weight through obscene gestures. This was the beginning of the conspiracy that ended with his death.

Nero's praetorian commander, Burrus, put up passive resistance against the unreasonable demands of the young ruler only once. His praetorians would protect the emperor in even the most unspeakable of escapades, but they refused to be accomplices to Agrippina's murder. This was a job left to the sailors of the imperial fleet and their freedmen captains.

When Burrus died in 62, Nero filled the position with two people, for reasons of security. The appointment of Faenius Rufus, who had previously been in charge of the grain supply, could evidently not be avoided. He received the position owing to his proven competent and incorruptible exercise of authority. The second, Ofonius Tigellinus, was Nero's preferred candidate. A man of dubious past from the circle of Caligula's sisters, he supported even the most extravagant wishes of the princeps.

Into the early 60s Nero could generally feel secure. The murder of his mother had not been forgotten among some of the praetorians, but this was not enough truly to jeopardize his position. Not until Burrus' death in 62 and Seneca's voluntary withdrawal from public life – which for many observers was an unsettling sign – was Nero tempted to live out his private artistic ambitions with increasing abandon. His public appearances as an artist and actor were considered a challenge and, for some status-conscious senators, almost as reprehensible as the matricide.

Nero had become convinced that the senatorial class could deal obediently with virtually anything, at most at the price of satirical verses – for which the penalty was banishment – or sour expressions at imperial festivals. Under the surface a change could be perceived in the stance of parts of the Roman ruling classes starting at the earliest around 62. At that time satirical verses about the princeps became known to the court and Thrasea Paetus, a senator regarded as particularly strict and irreproachable, intimated some of his criticism of the princeps in the Senate. The burning of Rome, combined with what many saw as Nero's inappropriate behavior in combating the blaze, must have been another factor contributing to the widespread discontent. Perhaps thoughts were already brewing at that time to make an attempt on the emperor's life.

A downright conspiracy against Nero with the goal of assassinating him and pronouncing a successor emerged in the lead-up to the celebration of the "Neronia" games planned for 65. In the eyes of the more conservative senators,

it could be assumed that the games would be a mockery
of all long-standing Roman traditions. It cannot totally be
ruled out that the renewed pregnancy of Poppaea aroused
additional fears, as the birth of an heir to the throne would
make Nero even more unbearable.

Those who became increasingly incensed over Nero's
manner were not interested in reestablishing the Republic.
They were more concerned about who, based on descent
and character, would be in a position to replace Nero and
at the same time be acceptable to the Senate.

Gaius Calpurnius Piso was a descendant of the Republican
aristocracy and had been forced into exile under Caligula.
He became a consul under Claudius and played a leading
role in the society of the capital. He was not one of Nero's
advisors and did not show any open political ambitions,
yet he spoke out for his clients in court in the style of his
forebears. He was regarded as generous but not wasteful
and he was friendly in his dealings with people he did not
know without seeming haughty. In contrast to Nero, Piso
even fit the male ideal of a nobleman. His household
signaled to the public that he was not a follower of any
ascetic doctrine and in keeping with the times he did not
shy from making public his – dilettantish – artistic talent
as an actor in tragedies through private performances. In a
certain way he embodied the Neronian zeitgeist in a way
that was acceptable even to those of stricter disposition.
Tacitus himself considered the nominal head of the conspiracy to be a weakling who would ultimately not prove
honorable to the glory of his ancestors.

As was his type, Piso did not push ahead at all. Tacitus
attached importance to the remarkable situation that the
conspiracy was started by praetorian officers who no longer
wanted to endure Nero's actions. The motives of this group
have been clearly recorded. Before his execution, Subrius
Flavas responded to Nero's question as to his motives for
breaking his oath of allegiance: "I hated you," he replied;
"yet not a soldier was more loyal to you while you deserved to be loved. I began to hate you when you became

the murderer of your mother and your wife, a charioteer, an actor, and an incendiary" (Tac. *Ann.* 15.67). This is an indication of the devastating impact that Nero's inappropriate behavior had on men with moral standards – and on women, including the freedwoman Epicharis, who remained loyal to her principles despite the torture. Some of the conspirators had very personal motives for participating. The poet Lucan, a nephew of Seneca, was said to have had his literary vanity offended, and Faenius Rufus, one of the two praetorian commanders, was supposedly simply afraid of his colleague Tigellinus, whom Nero favored. The circle of conspirators was quite wide: From the effeminate roué to the freedwoman with a past, there were many rather unexpected members of a conspiracy aiming to put things back on an orderly basis.

There was long discussion on how to carry out the deed. The best opportunity to kill Nero would be during one of his sojourns at Piso's villa at the Bay of Naples. Piso rejected this plan, supposedly because it was contrary to all laws of hospitality. However, critical observers felt that in fact Piso did not want to be so far away from the center of activities in Rome when Nero died. Ambitious as he had become, Piso feared the claims of the young Lucius Junius Silanus, who might have seemed attractive to some senators because of his somewhat stricter lifestyle, not to mention the fact that he was distantly related to Augustus. And he feared the consul Vestinus, who was even said to have Republican sympathies.

It was finally agreed to kill Nero during the *Ludi Ceriales* in April. During those circus games, Nero would leave his highly secured new palace, the *Domus Aurea*, to watch the races. The act was to be initiated similar to Caesar's murder on the Ides of March. Lateranus, known for his physical strength, would kneel before Nero as a petitioner and then grab hold of him. The other assassins among the praetorians would finish the job. Piso was to wait nearby for Faenius Rufus, who was supposed to bring him to the praetorian camp to be pronounced as the new princeps by the praetorians, just as Burrus had once announced the young Nero to the troops.

Vanity and weak nerves caused the conspirators to fail. The senator Flavius Scaevinus, who had just spent numerous hours conferring with Piso's closest confidant Natalis, aroused the curiosity of his freedman Milichus through his talkative parting mood. He had revised his will yet again and showered surprising testamentary provisions and gifts on his household staff. When his master's dagger also had to be resharpened, Milichus became suspicious and discussed the day's peculiarities with his wife. His pragmatic wife urged him that it would be advantageous for him to announce his observations as quickly as possible at court. Soon he was standing before Nero and explained all he knew.

Natalis and Scaevinus, masters of courageous talk, could not even stand to look at the instruments of torture and started naming names as fast as they could, perhaps even some who had nothing at all to do with the conspiracy. The fact that Seneca could now be drawn into the affair, presumably unjustly, must have particularly pleased Nero. For those who had been born free, torture was as a rule only threatened. This restraint did not apply for the freedwoman Epicharis. No torture could break her courage and silence, and in an unobserved moment she managed to kill herself, thus putting an end to her suffering.

A state of emergency was declared in Rome. Troops patrolled everywhere. The gravity of the situation was visible in that regular troops were joined by German bodyguards. The honest Faenius Rufus distinguished himself with particular zeal; though one of the most important conspirators, he had previously not aroused any suspicion at all. He did not bat an eyelash at the hearing when Subrius Flavus gesticulated wildly, wanting to get him to attack the emperor, who was standing next to him.

Piso, who had such great hopes of receiving the prime position in the polity, was virtually paralyzed in this situation. It was not simply by accident that Tacitus did not even mention him in his very detailed description. On the suggestion of confidants to appeal to the troops and the people of Rome to risk everything, Piso did nothing. He preferred to sit in his garden and await his arrest. He could see how much sense it would have made to appeal to the troops by looking at those who were stationed in front of his villa, waiting until he took his life. Only recruits and soldiers of low rank had been selected. Even the last will and testament of the man selected to be Nero's successor showed him to have been the wrong choice: His loathsome flattery of Nero was intended to protect his wife Atria Galla, whom he had wooed away from one of his friends.

Among the victims of Nero's revenge was Seneca. He had long since withdrawn from public life and avoided everything that could have attracted Nero's attention. It is improbable that Seneca was even indirectly involved in Piso's plans. Nero's suspicions had already been aroused when the loquacious conspirator Natalis announced that Piso had once been worried and had Seneca informed that he greatly regretted not seeing him any more. Nero immediately had Seneca interrogated in order to verify the statement; at that time he had been living on one of his estates not far from the capital.

Seneca's answer confirmed the version of the message to Piso as it had been cited during the interrogation of the conspirators. But Nero was no longer interested in exonerating his former teacher. Filled with rage he assumed Seneca's involvement in the conspiracy and was even supported in that by Tigellinus and Poppaea.

The death sentence was delivered by Gavius Silvanus, a praetorian officer who was himself part of the conspiracy. In hopes of saving his own life, he did not refuse the order, but he could not bring himself to read Seneca the death sentence in person. Instead, he sent a sergeant into Seneca's house. Seneca had no doubts that his death was inescapable. In his last hours of living and dying, stylized in the example set by Socrates, he profoundly impressed both contemporaries and posterity. He died as he had urged in his writings and no one had any doubt that life and teachings, or rather dying and teachings, were in impressive harmony. Thrasea Paetus, a victim of Nero in 66 and definitely critical toward Nero's ministers, oriented himself in the hour of his death toward Seneca. Tacitus, who had a sharp eye for all honesty and all hypocrisy, ended his report on Seneca's death with a note on his extremely simple burial, as Seneca had laid down in his will. He had written these stipulations when he was an undisputed minister of Nero, a time when he was among the most influential and wealthy men of Rome.

Later reports told of how cruel the interrogations had been, in which the accused almost collapsed under the weight of their doubled and tripled chains. At least nineteen men and women lost their lives in the aftermath of the conspiracy, and thirteen were banished into exile. The praetorians received a lavish gift of money in reward for their now somewhat questionable loyalty. In Nero's view, three men had been chiefly responsible for quashing the conspiracy; they received, as a reward as it were for military achievements of the highest rank, the "ornamenta triumphalia": Tigellinus, Cocceius Nerva (later, in 96, he also became a respectable princeps for two years), and the incumbent consul Petronius Turpilianus, who would still be loyal to Nero in 68.

His loyalty notwithstanding, the vigilant Tigellinus was not permitted to lead the praetorians on his own. His new colleague was a man whom Nero was certain would be unscrupulous. Up to then Nymphidius Sabinus had made a career as a praetorian officer. He enjoyed the aura he created as an illegitimate son of Caligula and made a great effort to emphasize a certain sinister similarity with his supposed begetter.

Nero's pleasure at the Senate's decree to name the month of his birth "Neronius" will have been short-lived. He became increasingly aware of the opposition in leading circles. Even minor signs of intellectual independence became sufficient grounds for being dragged to court. In 65 Nero's last conceivable dynastic rival was killed. The young Lucius Junius Silanus Torquatus, son of Silanus who had been murdered in 51, was one generation further removed from Augustus than Nero was.

In Nero's final years there was another, more indirect form of opposition that Nero began to fear no less than the one that had led to plans for his assassination. Members of this passive – and precisely for this reason publicly perceptible – opposition are usually referred to as stoics, though not all of those in the so-called "Stoic opposition" could unreservedly be considered adherents of this philosophical school. Stoics had no difficulty accepting a principate with its well-ordered, Augustan structure. No Stoic doctrine explicitly incited opposition to the new state form. On the contrary, some professed Stoics had been advisors to Hellenistic royal courts. Seneca himself followed Stoic doctrine and long considered his philosophical credo to be compatible with his activities for Nero. Stoic philosophy could even have been declared the "official" state philosophy.

But Nero was the first princeps who felt threatened by Stoic philosophy because of the political influence of those who articulated their criticism in the spirit of Stoicism. The most well known of these regime critics who was rebuked as a doctrinaire Stoic, by their opponents at least, was Thrasea Paetus. He was condemned to death in 66, not long before Nero traveled to Greece. Thrasea Paetus belonged not to the senatorial high nobility, but to the social climbers from northern Italy who prided themselves on their conservative principles. He might have owed his entrance to the Senate to Agrippina. Seneca was one of his supporters and in 56 Thrasea served as a consul for three months. He and his friends did not oppose the principate; instead, they gauged Nero by his policy statement of 51, according to which he wanted to respect the usual division of power between princeps and Senate. The successful social climber thus carried out the role of a senator with far greater zeal than the remaining aristocrats from the great families.

Nero might not have felt physically threatened by this type of critic, but he had every reason to fear for his already damaged reputation among the senators. After Nero refused to receive Thrasea's felicitations on the birth of his daughter Claudia Augusta in 63, Thrasea attended senatorial sessions only very seldom. His withdrawal from political life as a form of protest was not punishable, but his behavior raised a stir beyond the borders of the city. Nero considered it a silent reproach that must have reminded him of the broken promises of the policy statement of 51. This behavior was stoic at most in its unwavering insistence on policies that had once been declared right and proper.

Nero arranged that a personal adversary of Thrasea declare this behavior in the Senate to be high treason and demand a commensurate penalty. During the proceedings, the Senate was surrounded by troops. The verdict against Thrasea brought the death penalty and his son-in-law Helvidius Priscus, who was no less loyal to his convictions, was banished into exile.

Thrasea abstained from having a defense in the Senate, preferring to await the pronouncement of the expected verdict at home. He stylized his death in the manner of Socrates; his last conversation was with a philosopher about the immortality of the soul. He showed remarkable consistency in not making a single statement against the princeps. Thrasea's words to the quaestor who had to deliver the death sentence became his political legacy; he admonished steadfastness ("*constantia*") but not active resistance against the tyrant. No one in the Senate had any opportunity to come to Thrasea's aid, but he was considered a "martyr" in the struggle against the *tyrannus*. For posterity Thrasea was certainly on a par with Caesar's opponent Cato, about whom he had written a biography.

Criticism of Nero in the final years of his rule sometimes took on very unexpected forms. One of his masters of good or even more doubtful taste had long been Gaius Petronius. Privately a roué of utmost cunning, he was nevertheless a competent consul and provincial administrator.

Tigellinus' enmity toward him proved Petronius' demise in 66. After his sentence had become inevitable he met death with a parody on the death of Socrates, not by speaking about philosophical questions as his strength began to ebb, but by continuing his usual light conversation. As a final greeting to Nero he did not fill his will with flatteries, as other victims of Nero had invented in an effort to save at least some of their fortunes for their descendants. Instead, he wrote a personal letter to the princeps listing all the sexual extravagances that Nero fancied.

Nero's heedless actions against alleged and actual opponents in the years 65 and 66 can be explained primarily as being caused by his increasing insecurity and due to advisors such as Nymphidius and Tigellinus. At the same time Nero and his advisors might have also been thinking about the trip to Greece that had long been planned, which was possibly going to be followed by a campaign in the Caucasus. Whether planned or not, as far as one could judge Nero had not left behind any critics of rank for the time of his absence. And for many, hopes for positions of command took the place of criticism. Not until it was absolutely clear that the praetorians had abandoned Nero did opposition reappear in Rome.

X

Trip to Greece

Nero considered the summer of 66 to be the best time to complete serious preparations for the long-planned journey to Greece. The Pisonian conspiracy of the previous year had been thwarted. By summer 66 at the latest the irritating Thrasea Paetus was dead, as was the last presumed rival from the family of the Silani. Even the underage son from the first marriage of his wife Poppaea had been eliminated. And Antonia, Claudius' daughter and thus a good catch for an adversary with political ambitions, had also had to die.

An attempt at a coup in the style of the Pisonian conspiracy was not to be feared for the time being. After Tiridates' visit in early 66, Nero enjoyed a certain degree of popularity. In Rome people would recall the celebrations of the new policies on the eastern provinces and be sympathetic toward the emperor's interest in further securing Rome's position in the world. The enthusiastic welcome he could reckon with in the east would continue to weaken any oppositional thoughts, if indeed any remained, in his surroundings. And he could feel safe from attack within the circle of his praetorian guard.

The decision to set off in September 66 was not a quick, let alone spontaneous, one. The journey was planned to last two years. The sudden return to Rome in late 67 makes it easy to forget how long the emperor had been planning to be away from the capital. Long before September 66 court directives must have been sent to the eastern provinces.

Construction measures existed for Olympia and for Corinth, where Nero planned to have his Greek headquarters. Thermal baths for visits by the emperor were built in Alexandria; the Alexandrian coins naming the relevant destinations of the emperor show how meticulously the "public relations work" for the east had been organized.

Political affairs were to be managed in Nero's absence by the freedmen Helius and Polyclitus, assisted by Nymphidius Sabinus. Nero left behind an intimidated Senate that had been robbed of many important personalities. Observers noted that the senatorial delegation was not honored with any ceremonial farewell kiss. The senators accompanying him certainly had not all volunteered to be part of his entourage, yet neither were his fellow travelers all hostages or flatterers. The respected Cluvius Rufus, for example, offered his services voluntarily. He was not suspected of any disloyalty and preferred to spend his time writing books about acting.

Tigellinus and his praetorians assured the safety of the princeps, and a selected delegation of claques, the so-called Augustiani, was responsible for his applause. Surprisingly, Nero's new wife Statilia Messalina, whom he had just married in early 66, stayed home. His personal well-being was looked after by the scandalous eunuch Sporus, who supposedly closely resembled his beloved Poppaea. The care of Sporus was entrusted to the sinister Calvia Crispinilla, who was best informed about all the peculiarities of the court.

Nero informed the Greeks in advance that he wanted to compete in all the important festivals, each of which took place in its own four-year cycle. His greatest wish led to a change in the usual festival schedule. Nero thus had an opportunity to participate in the games at Olympia, Delphi, the Isthmus of Corinth, and Nemea within one year. It was his express wish to return as a *"periodonikes,"* a victor in all four panhellenic games.

After the crossing Nero arrived on Corfu and gave his first performance. He then made a point of traveling to Actium in honor of Apollo, whom Augustus had admired, and to prove that his philhellene endeavors referred not only to his grandfather Germanicus but to Augustus himself. He wintered in Corinth.

Nero spent the year 67 as a participant in the major festivals. Not only was the schedule of the festivals changed for his sake, in Olympia for example, but also their repertoire, which had remained the same since time immemorial. The emperor was to be given the chance to participate in all disciplines he desired. At the Isthmian Games in Corinth he was therefore allowed to compete for the newly established prize for acting, and in Olympia a new competition was also added, offering prizes for actors and kitharodes. The emperor seems to have taken all of these competitions very seriously. True to the style he let his hair grow down the back of his neck. He was very excited during his performances and felt like one competitor among many. Nero did not seem to notice the nervousness of the judges who knew what was expected of them. He could definitely use his performances in the eastern provinces, which often felt neglected by "Italy" and "the West," to gain popularity. The prefect of Egypt felt it was appropriate to publicize Nero's victories on coins.

His travels – and the history of the dynasty – almost came to an unexpected end when Nero insisted on personally driving a ten-horse team. It was not enough for him to have a professional chariot racer harness the horses on his behalf, as Tiberius had preferred when he was heir to the throne (that is, with the approval of Augustus), and later Germanicus in the year 17. Nero barely survived a bad fall and was revived by his joy over being awarded first prize despite his accident.

Nero is said to have won 1,808 prizes in all and he sent some of them on ahead back to Italy. The judges were rewarded for their friendly appraisal; they received Roman civil rights, which were awarded by tradition very sparingly, and a handsome sum of money. Nero was particularly proud of the laurels he had won in Olympia and Delphi. When he later entered Rome as a "victor" he was wearing the Olympic laurels on his head and carrying the Delphic in his right hand. His vanity became increasingly odd; the freedman Helius had the senator Sulpicius Camerinus executed because he would not give up the cognomen "Pythicus," which had been part of his family tradition, since now only Nero was to be entitled to that name, as victor at the Pythian games at Dephi.

If aside from the satisfied judges there were other Greeks who had hopes of financial gain from the visit of the emperor they were occasionally disappointed. Nero took the games seriously, but he took the usual victory prizes just as seriously. Unfazed, he really did accept the prize moneys he was awarded, and as a connoisseur he insisted on appropriating the most beautiful works of art for the imperial collection.

Extant sources focus on the emperor's extravagant performances but it cannot be ruled out that Nero intended to have some impact in promoting Greek culture in the *Imperium Romanum*. Even early observers remarked that the philhellene Nero did not visit Athens and Sparta. Perhaps the Corinthians showered him with such flattery and celebrations that of all the "great" cities he wanted to honor only Corinth with his presence, respecting the Corinthians' local rivalry with Athens and Sparta. It is also conceivable, however, that behind the superficial preference of Corinth, Nero promoted the concept of a "Roman" rather than a "classical" Greece, as a true part of the empire and not merely as a province.

Nero definitely knew how to increase his popularity lastingly in Greece, beyond merely receiving applause in the theater. In November 67 – that is, after his successful tour of the cities holding games – he staged the magnificent "liberation of Greece" from tax burdens and Roman jurisdiction. In a small city in Boeotia an inscription has survived with the words of Nero's speech to the Greeks gathered in the Corinthian theater (he had just won first prize as a herald in Olympia). It is important evidence of Nero's effusive oratory style in the final months of his life.

At the time he had become increasingly convinced of his own incomparable significance and the divine protection he felt was befitting of him. The constant flattery from the Greeks encouraged him by reinforcing this heightened self-perception:

Imperator Caesar proclaims: "Since I wish to reward most noble Greece for its good will and piety towards me, I order that as many as possible from this province attend at Corinth on November 29th." When crowds had gathered in convention, he delivered the following address:

"Men of Greece, I bestow upon you an unexpected gift – though anything may be anticipated from my generosity – a gift of such a size that you were incapable of asking for it. All you Greeks who inhabit Achaea and what until now was the Peloponnese, receive freedom and immunity from taxation, something you have not all had even in your most prosperous times, for you have been slaves either to foreigners or to each other. I wish that I might have bestowed this gift when Greece was at her peak, so that more might enjoy my beneficence. For this reason I hold the times to blame for having reduced the size of my beneficence. But, as it is, I bestow beneficence upon you not out of pity but out of good will and I reward your gods, whose constant care for me on land and sea I have enjoyed, because they have made it possible for me to bestow such great benefactions. For other principes have conferred freedom on cities, but only Nero has done so even on a province." (Dessau, ILS 8794 = Braund, no. 261)

The "freedom of Greece" was a phrase used with alternating success in the struggle to win public support among the Greeks; it never let go of the nostalgic memories of the great epochs of their past. A fitting example of this mentality is the name of the Theban dignitary who in the small Boeotian city was responsible for the expected bombastic address of thanks to the distant Nero. His name was that of no one less than Epaminondas, the greatest Theban statesman in the fourth century BCE.

Achaea thus was given its freedom, and it was intended that the Peloponnese would be renamed after the princeps as soon as possible. That explains the "until now" at the mention of the name Peloponnese. The gift of freedom to the Greeks did not last long. Vespasian took advantage of local unrest to take back Greece's freedom. As an act of "philhellenism," however, Nero's act of liberation made a surprisingly profound impression on the Greek populace. Even the plundering of the art collections for the benefit of the imperial household thereby faded into the background. Later Greek authors such as Plutarch and Pausanias mentioned the freedom for Greece in order – as they said – to let Nero enjoy a bit of justice.

Nero did not leave it at this presentation of Greek liberty, which did not cost much since the taxes of the province Achaea were insignificant anyway. His interest in daring hydraulic engineering projects is well documented for Italy within the context of improving the system of food distribution. Now he felt inspired to cut a canal through the Isthmus of Corinth as a gift to Greece.

This undertaking was one of the great commerce and trade projects for Greece that had been considered again and again over centuries by daring planners wanting to make it possible to avoid the difficult rounding of the Peloponnese. Demetrios Poliorketes had spoken of it in the third century BCE; Caesar had commissioned the job (without the plan being ridiculed) and Caligula wanted to match him. Now this was how Nero intended to render outstanding services to the Greeks and to trade.

Work began in 67 after Greece had been "liberated"; with a golden spade he had received from the hands of the former procurator, Nero dug out the first bit of earth. The work was done not by the artistic Greeks, but by 6,000 Jewish prisoners of war who had been captured by Vespasian, the new commander in Judea. Perhaps even praetorians were ordered to take spades in their hands, a job that would not have made them feel very honored. About one-fifth of the total distance of almost four miles was dug out. Vespasian and later emperors no longer considered the project to be worth the engineering effort, since they faced structural difficulties. Not until 1897 was the canal across the isthmus completed.

With all these distractions, Nero still had time to ensure his own safety, and he remained surrounded by enough people whose own welfare was dependent on his survival. Helius, his imperial deputy in Rome, kept the peace through intimidating arrests and by executing innocent people. By that time Nero saw the Senate as nothing but an obstacle. When he announced his congratulations and blessings as he dug out the first shovelful for the isthmus he spoke only of himself and the Roman people but not, as would have been usual, of the Senate.

After hearing reports of a conspiracy by Vinicianus, a son-in-law of Corbulo the commander in the eastern provinces, Nero invited Corbulo most flatteringly to Corinth. It is notable that Corbulo accepted the compliments at face value and he might have hoped for an honorable reception or even a promotion. But when he was barred from visiting the emperor after arriving in the port of Corinth Corbulo finally understood the hopelessness of his situation. He could obviously not count on any help. His last remaining option was to commit suicide before it came to official charges, which would have brought an inevitable confiscation of his family fortune. At that time Nero preferred to rely on commanders like Vespasian, whose relatively humble background would rule out any greater political ambitions.

Nero's treatment of Corbulo and the commanders of the Rhine army, the Scribonius brothers, is a sign of the virtually unshakeable power of a princeps from the family of Augustus. The brothers were both denounced to Nero for unknown reasons and embarked on the long journey from the Rhine to Corinth to plead their defense. They had to die as Corbulo had.

This and other events, such as grain ships not arriving or military wages not being paid, appeared to have destabilized the situation in Rome. Helius continued to summon help and when none of his dispatches brought any action, he took off himself in the middle of winter, despite the unfavorable sailing weather.

Helius' arrival in Greece was not appreciated, since Nero was in the midst of pursuing great, almost fantastical plans, only the contours of which can be made out today. He intended to dedicate himself to military undertakings after completing his journey as a *periodonikes* in order to gain the military prestige he was still lacking. Sources report of preparations for a campaign at the northeastern border of the empire, in the Caucasus or Black Sea region. Reports on simultaneous plans for a military campaign to Ethiopia have also survived, but it is not clear how the two projects were supposed to be linked chronologically. It had in any case already been announced that Nero would be traveling to Alexandria.

A division of praetorians had received orders in advance to scout out the march route to Ethiopia. The Roman troops in Egypt were already increased by 2,000 men in 66. Auxiliary troops, including German cavalry, were moved out toward Egypt. The military goal of such an undertaking is difficult to ascertain; in any case Nero could have reported of an extremely exotic, largely unknown theater of war where not even Alexander the Great had been.

More realistic are the reports of plans for a campaign around the northeastern border of the empire. Tacitus spoke expressly of a war that Nero planned against the Albanians ("Albani"), as they are referred to in the ancient text, a people at the Caspian Sea. More than a hundred years earlier Pompeius had waged war against them. There is every reason to believe that Tacitus, as Theodor Mommsen presumed, meant the Alans ("Alani"), a people in the region of present-day Georgia, north of Tiflis. This would have been a matter of securing the northern coast of the Black Sea and the adjacent regions, which for several years had been suffering invasions by impoverished barbarian tribes. This emulation of Alexander could have also played a role

Figure 8 Late portrait of Nero (Munich, Glyptothek 321). BPK Berlin. Photo: Alfredo Dagli Orti

here: Nero was only thirty-one years old and absolutely healthy despite all his excesses, as amazed observers reported. In Italy he had a new legion of "long fellows" levied; they had to be at least six feet tall, which was unusual for legionnaires.

It never came to a serious test of Nero's military capabilities in these campaigns; he certainly would have sorely missed Corbulo's experience. Helius' report on the situation in Rome left Nero no other choice but to interrupt his trip and return. In December 67 or a little later he set foot on Italian soil again.

The well-planned return of the victor did not let it show that it was earlier than intended. Nero obviously was not in a hurry. The *periodonikes* did not travel directly to Rome, despite Helius' reports of a catastrophic situation. Instead he let himself be celebrated in Naples, the city of his first own artistic performance. In the style of the victors of games from days past he entered the city on a chariot drawn by white horses through a path cut in the city wall. With similar ado he also entered Antium, Alba, and finally Rome, evidently unhindered by the unrest that Helius had reported. Nero set an unusual "philhellene" accent by entering Rome on Augustus' triumphal chariot. He presented himself like a triumphator from the kingdom of the Muses. He wore the dress of a real – military – triumphator, albeit extravagantly modified. The tablets that were carried during the procession did not list the names of conquered peoples and cities, as in ancient times; inscribed were instead the names of those he had beaten in the artistic competitions as well as a list of his repertoire. Senators and knights dutifully participated in the procession; following the chariot of the victor were also claques from his trip to Greece instead of the battle-tried soldiers that usually followed the chariot of a triumphator. The historian Cassius Dio cited the chorus chanting to please the victor:

Hail, Olympian Victor! Hail, Pythian Victor! Augustus! Augustus! Hail to Nero, our Hercules! Hail to Nero, our Apollo! The only Victor of the Grand Tour, the only one from the beginning of time! Augustus! Augustus! O, Divine Voice! Blessed are they that hear thee. (Cassius Dio 63.20 (5))

The destination of the triumphal march in the past had been the temple of Jupiter on the Capitoline. Nero took a different route to the temple of Apollo on the Palatine Hill to thank his tutelary god. Everything stood in a strange contrast to the planned campaigns in the south and northeast, which must have been discussed at the time. In the evening he had his many prizes and the statues showing him in artistic poses set up in his bedchamber. The "triumphal procession" was followed by many other festivities and performances, in which the emperor supposedly even let someone else win once, in order to lend more credibility to the honesty of his Greek victories. Nero did not stay in Rome for long, especially since – having received such choruses – he evidently no longer feared any unrest. A short time after these festivals he returned to Naples to practice his art.

XI

The End of the Dynasty

———

By the year 68 Nero had managed to see that no one was still alive who could trace their heritage either directly or indirectly back to Augustus. After all the events of the previous years, now no one stood in his way. If he therefore felt secure it was in no way irrational. Tacitus, who had carefully studied the events at the end of Nero's reign, stressed that Nero's fall was due far less to the strength of his opponents than to his own mistakes.

The first reports of a revolt in the west supposedly reached Nero in Naples on March 20 or 21, the anniversary of his mother's death (the Romans loved paying attention to such coincidences). If anyone had expected Nero to panic, they were mistaken. He did not let himself be fazed; in fact his reaction led many to believe that he wanted to take advantage of the announcements in order to plunder the western provinces even more than he already had. He paid particular attention to the athletic competitions, in which he occasionally acted as if he were a knowledgeable judge or coach. The messengers who kept coming with bad reports from Gaul met with his anger. If the reports that he did not respond to any dispatches from the west for eight days are accurate, then it is obvious that Nero was suffering from delusions of grandeur, acting as though the popularity he had enjoyed in the previous months in the east had made him invulnerable.

His "artistry" became increasingly absurd. The problem that concerned him most in the final weeks of his reign was taking care of his voice for future performances. He even delegated others to give important speeches, even appeals or daily commands to the praetorians. If there was absolutely no way around his making a personal statement, his speech coach stood next to him to prevent him from straining his voice.

Corbulo had accepted his fate without resistance the previous year. If Nero chose to interpret the initial announcements of the fall of Gaius Julius Vindex, the governor of the province of Gallia Lugdunensis, as merely a welcome opportunity to plunder Gaul as punishment, it is almost understandable. Vindex was not a member of the Roman aristocracy. He was a descendant of a high-ranking Celtic family from Aquitania. He could count on support when planning his rebellion against the exploitation of Gaul through Nero's taxation demands. Such a following was due not only to his status as a Roman senator, but also because of his descent from Aquitania's old ruling class. Later reporters sometimes referred to him as the Celtic "nationalist" against Rome, but this does not concur with the coins that show him calling for the liberation of the entire Roman world from the tyrant. But Vindex was not the man who could get the commanders of the Rhine army to put aside their fear for their lives and participate in a revolt, despite all that Nero had already done. Most of those who received information about Vindex' plans obsequiously passed the news on to Rome.

Servius Sulpicius Galba, an elderly man of 73 years and a Republican nobleman, was a governor in Spain. He was sometimes said to have a well-concealed ambition. He had of course avoided a marriage proposal from Agrippina in the year 41. Since 60 he had acted appropriately as governor in one of the Spanish provinces (Hispania Tarraconensis) and was cautiously concerned with living as long as possible. He always traveled with a second carriage filled with gold coins, just in case he had to leave the country on short notice. Of all the governors in 68 he was the only one that Nero would have had to fear in view of his descent, although he was not related to Augustus. Instead, he could refer only to having had enjoyed being a protégé of Livia, wife of Augustus. He was evidently one of the few who had not reported to Nero immediately about the riots in the west, which thus explains the news that in March or a short time later Nero commissioned to have Galba murdered.

Vindex did not only ask Galba for support, as he had also asked the other governors; because of Galba's undisputed reputation Vindex also urged him to lead the revolt and declare himself Nero's successor. Galba did not agree to do this until a failed attempt on his life convinced him that he was compromised in Nero's eyes anyway. The support of two other officials in the west – Otho, governor of Lusitania, and Aulus Caecina Alienus, quaestor in the province of Hispania Baetica – were reason enough for him to become more active, albeit with reservations. A declaration of April 2, 68 against Nero was still cautiously worded. At the marketplace of New Carthage, surrounded by pictures of Nero's victims and accompanied by a young man who had to eke out an existence in exile on the Balearic Islands, he complained generally about the bad times and evidently relied especially on the language of the images. The arranged cheers for the Imperator came quickly, but he was still not willing to accept the succession from Nero. He preferred to be called the "legate of the Senate and People of Rome." Yet the fact that he was levying troops at the same time made it clear that he was serious.

Galba had spent eight years avoiding anything that could have aroused Nero's suspicions, so he was virtually crushed when he received news in May that Verginius Rufus, the governor of Upper Germany, had defeated Vindex' troops near Besançon (Vesontio). It is not known what directly led up to this battle. Verginius was not one of the princeps's admirers, but neither did he abandon Nero at the first opportunity that arose. There is every reason to believe that Verginius Rufus was still loyal at that time. Later, when he was highly respected under the Flavians, his unexpectedly long-lived loyalty was mercifully concealed under a cloak of silence.

The battle between the legionnaires from Upper Germany and Vindex' largely Celtic troops at Vesontio might not trace back to clear orders from Verginius. It might have developed out of the lack of discipline and greed of Vindex' troops, who wanted to feel superior to the still loyal troops of Verginius. If Verginius and Vindex had indeed negotiated with each other on the possibility of joining forces to continue the fight against Nero, they would not have been able to rely on their troops. The spoils of war were far more important to the legionnaires than the struggle of the two high-ranking men against the distant Nero.

When Vindex sought to commit suicide after his defeat, Verginius reasonably declined the title of Imperator that he was offered. A governor of knightly descent from northern Italy was the worst conceivable candidate for the highest position of power.

Galba's despair over the news from Vesontio shows how strong he still considered Nero's position. The consuls Rubrius Gallus and Petronius Turpilianus were in northern Italy. They had already proven themselves to be absolutely reliable during the Pisonian conspiracy. And other troops from Illyricum had received marching orders and had not mutinied.

If Nero had only had the courage, for example, to go immediately to the troops in northern Italy and take the initiative, things would presumably have gone very differently. Nero did not take advantage of his opportunity. He failed, as always, when he got into difficulties and lacked advisors of the caliber of a Burrus or Seneca.

Nero heard about Vindex' disloyalty in Naples. He tried to keep news of the rebellion quiet for a whole week. But Vindex knew how he could reach the public in Italy and Rome. Pamphlets came from the west, harshly worded to hurt Nero's vanity. Quite in the sense of the senatorial critics, Vindex referred to the princeps as a wretched zither player, addressing Nero – as Britannicus had earlier – with his birth name Ahenobarbus.

The ridicule of his artistry hit Nero harder than any military threat to his rule. Although he had spent the previous months refusing any serious contact with the Senate, now his hurt pride inspired him to write to the senators, calling for them to punish Vindex for his insults. He repeatedly sought confirmation from his surroundings that Vindex was totally unjustified in dragging his artistic talent through the mud.

During these decisive months it was apparent that Nero increasingly lost his nerve. The thirty-one-year-old princeps fluctuated between depression and wishful thinking. When unexpectedly good news once came, he barely managed to turn mocking verses about the leader of the revolt, accompanied by suggestive hand movements. There was no one left who was willing to give him good advice. His nurses are mentioned once as comforters in time of need and it was they who also buried him. It is known that during these final weeks Nymphidius Sabinus, one of the two praetorian prefects, turned against Nero in time to save himself. Tigellinus, Nero's evil spirit of past years, was not around due to illness and the energetic Poppaea was dead. In his despair the ruler even turned to the art of the Etruscan haruspices, prophesying by examining animal entrails, but it was not able to calm him with favorable results.

Anyone at court who read Vindex' pamphlets had to admit that at this time of crisis the princeps was truly more a bad zither player than a dignified holder of the highest office. High-ranking senators who were evidently still loyal were summoned to a consultation on countermeasures, but after a brief discussion of the situation they had to listen to a presentation on a new type of water organ. It was around this time that Nero publicly vowed that after defeating his adversary he would appear not only as a kitharode, as he had previously, but also as an organ virtuoso and flautist, as a bagpiper, and, last but not least, as a ballet dancer. And he was even prepared to play the socially least respected part of a dancer and pantomime in public. A remark he supposedly made – which, if not authentic then at least very inventive – was that if all else failed he could support himself as an artist.

Even such statements should perhaps be viewed as a demonstration of Nero's disdain of Vindex' revolt. However, the news of Galba's breach of loyalty, which reached Rome in mid-April at the latest, shows that the situation had really got out of control. Galba was a serious rival despite – or because of – his advanced age. Nero's old friend Otho, whom he had sent to Lusitania many years earlier to keep him from disturbing Nero's relationship with Poppaea, was already hoping to be adopted by the childless elderly gentleman who was preparing to succeed Nero.

Some of the reports on the last weeks of Nero's reign are so lurid as to allow doubts as to their credibility. There were loyal troops in northern Italy and additional soldiers were on their way there. Nero supposedly decided in the end to approach the rebels, but Suetonius' notes on the subject read more like the products of a vivid imagination. Is it possible that Nero was really concerned only with his musical equipment, the transportation for the ladies of his court, and the presumably authentic costumes of an Amazon corps?

Reports of orders in the last days to levy troops even in Rome itself seem more realistic. In previous times of crisis that was always a sign of the direst of straits. The situation was evidently already so bad that the potential recruits could evade the orders. Nero's attempt to muster suitable slaves must be seen as an acknowledgment of the impending disaster. It is also true that Nero ordered that a tax be paid only in gold and silver coins, with the additional stipulation that only freshly hallmarked coins would be accepted. The value of new and used coins was the same, however – did the artist want to see only "beautiful" coins?

More and more people abandoned the princeps. The actions of the two praetorian prefects in his close circle made his isolation obvious. There is nothing at all in the extant records about Ofonius Tigellinus' position; he was presumably ill. It is known that Nymphidius Sabinus thought only of his own future during these weeks. He had experienced Nero's failing leadership abilities close-up and acted accordingly. The Senate's recognition of Claudius' appointment by the praetorians in 41 had already shown the role that the clever use of the praetorian guards could play in the struggle for power.

In the final weeks of his reign, Nero made preparations for a very special attraction; he wanted to appear as a lion tamer in the role of Hercules. A lion had already been trained not to resist when the princeps attempted to choke it. His real opponents behaved differently. News of Vindex' suicide and Verginius' caution presumably never reached Nero, since he considered his situation in early June to be hopeless. On June 9 the Senate pronounced Galba to be the new princeps and Nero was condemned to death.

At that time military might in Rome was in the hands of Nymphidius Sabinus. He negotiated with the Senate on the loyalty of the praetorian troops. At the same time he declared his colleague Tigellinus to be the main offender as regards the excesses of recent years and permitted charges against some of the especially hated freedmen at court. Nymphidius himself was evidently still not totally convinced of Galba's success, as he spoke during these days in June of being an illegitimate son of Caligula, with all the corresponding associations.

On the night when Nero requested to no avail a military escort for his escape, Nymphidius announced the princeps' alleged escape plans in the praetorian camp. The senators who accompanied the prefects made it clear to even the most reluctant officers that the princeps had now run out of options. For any soldiers who still did not think Nero's total failure in the recent weeks was sufficient grounds to ignore the oath sworn on the princeps and his house, the change in rulers was made more bearable through the enormous cash gift that Nymphidius promised the praetorians in the name of the princeps Galba: ten years' wages (Nero had paid half that amount at the beginning of his reign).

Suetonius' reports of Nero's final hours are remarkably detailed, albeit lacking any possibility for their verification. The meticulous biographer nevertheless appears to have had no doubt as to the reliability of his sources.

On the same night that Nymphidius appeared in the praetorian camp, Nero received new reports of the defection of the troops and decided once and for all to flee. Perhaps he wanted to ask Galba for mercy; perhaps he wanted to go to the Parthians. The rooms of the palace gradually emptied. Only a few freedmen and the loyal Locusta were there with him; from her he had received a bottle of poison, just in case. His orders were carried out with growing reluctance. Someone supposedly called to him, "Is it so dreadful a thing then to die?" (Suet., *Nero*, 47–49). A draft of a speech was later found that Nero wanted to present to the people of Rome. He wanted to ask for forgiveness for past crimes or to be left the prefecture of Egypt. Thus he thought to the very end of his trip to Alexandria. His fear of being killed on the way to the Forum made him hesitate. He postponed the speech for the next day.

At midnight he received a message that the praetorian unit on duty had withdrawn from the palace; at least no praetorian had been found to carry out the death penalty. Nero was now almost alone in his palace. He knocked on the chamber doors of those who had always appreciated being allowed to live in the direct vicinity of the emperor, but found no one. When he returned to his own chamber, even his personal servants had left, but not without taking his costly blankets and even Locusta's vial of poison. The palace gladiators, who were always to be on call for special tasks, had also disappeared. Even his reliable bodyguard Spicillus, a former gladiator, was no longer there for Nero to ask to give him his death. "Have I then neither friend nor foe?" Nero is said to have called out.

Only very few did not abandon him. The freedman Phaon, who had been responsible in previous years for the finances of the empire, offered him a place to hide in his villa near Rome. Nero set out with four escorts, including Sporus. As the group passed through the streets, he could make out voices. "These men are after Nero," and another asked, "Is there anything new in the city about Nero?" When Nero's horse shied and in the excitement his face was no longer concealed a praetorian veteran recognized him and gave him a military salute.

It was not easy but Nero finally reached the estate. Phaon thought it wise for his refugee to arrive inconspicuously and had him sent at first to an underground hiding place. Nero rejected that, saying he would not go underground while he was still alive. He also rejected the moldy bread he was offered, but he did quench his great thirst. Self-pitying, he compared the puddle water he was first offered with the luxurious beverage made of snow, which he had enjoyed at court.

It was part of the aristocratic manner of the Roman elite to die honorably in hopeless situations before being killed at the hands of an executioner. Many of Nero's victims of previous years had taken their own lives, thereby ennobling themselves yet more. Everyone knew how Seneca, Thrasea Paetus, and Petronius had died. And it was also remembered when men who had paraded earnest principles in life had lost their stature in the face of death, as some of the members of the Pisonian conspiracy had done – especially Calpurnius Piso himself.

The last faithful followers could think of no better advice for Nero than to take his own life and thus avoid a disgraceful end. A burial site was quickly dug out, much more pathetic even than his mother's grave. When the grave was ready, Nero could be heard only sobbing. Here is where he is to have spoken his famous words, which – if authentic – are a key sign to Nero's image of himself in the final years of his rule: "*Qualis artifex pereo!*" (What a loss for the world of the theater!).

Messengers of Phaon arrived with the news of the proclamation of the Senate declaring Nero to be an enemy of the state and sentencing him to death "in the ancient fashion," that is, he was to be whipped to death. Even knowing the cruel manner in which he was to be executed did not suffice in strengthening Nero's resolve. Again and again he hesitated to use one of his two daggers. He preferred to think about the dirge he requested of Sporus, whom he thus had assigned the role of a woman at his funeral. Not until he could hear the arrival of a cavalry unit of the praetorians did Nero accept that there would be no way out. Epaphroditos, one of his freedmen ministers, helped him hold the dagger which he jabbed into his neck.

The praetorian who encountered the dying Nero did not have the courage to openly follow his orders to arrest him. Instead he pretended to want to take care of his wound. "This is fidelity!" were supposedly Nero's final words.

No one seriously reckoned with Nero's arrest. Icelus, a freedman of Galba, had been arrested at the beginning of Galba's proclamation but in the meantime had been released and was invested with making important decisions on behalf of his master. He ordered that Nero's body not be further defiled. The deceased was to be buried simply, without much ado, but with decency. That was not a sentimental decision; everyone knew that Nero still had followers among the people of the city of Rome.

As an "enemy of the state" Nero could not be buried in the mausoleum of Augustus. Instead, after he was cremated his urn was brought to the family grave of the Domitii, in the end justifying Britannicus' persistence in calling Nero by his birth family name. The cost of the funeral, still a substantial 200,000 sesterces, was paid for by Acte, who is mentioned at this point in the records for the first time after more than ten years, and his nurses Ecloge and Alexandria. Nero's ashes were placed in a coffin of crimson marble. After only a few weeks flowers were laid down at his grave and his memory became politically opportune.

XII

Quo Vadis? Nero's "Afterlife"

The contradictory statements about Nero's final hours quickly gave rise to rumors that he was in reality not dead at all, but was preparing his triumphant – and this time truly military – return to Rome. There were evidently groups that had some interest in spreading such rumors. Galba did not have the slightest doubt that the urban masses of Rome missed Nero's generous expenditures. This is also shown by Otho's and Vitellius' efforts to publicly demonstrate their honorable commemoration of their predecessor.

The first "false" Nero created unrest in Asia Minor at the time of Galba's rule. He came from the underclasses whose favor the genuine Nero carried through his benevolent deeds. He was a man of uncertain background, presumably a freedman from Italy who resembled Nero to some degree – the thick hair of an artist is mentioned. And of course he was not without talent as a singer and musician. His followers were made up largely of runaway slaves who gave the propertied class good reason to be terrified. There were enough people who definitely felt it was possible that Nero did in fact manage to escape from Italy. After the false Nero was arrested and executed, the body was put on display in the cities of Asia Minor as it was transported to Italy, in order to dispel any lingering doubts about Nero's "return."

While the longing for Nero to return might have been limited in Rome to the profiteers of the old regime and the less thoughtful theater and arena guests, the situation in the eastern part of the empire was very different. Nero continued to enjoy true popularity there even after he died. This can be explained in part by the profound disgruntlement among even the upper classes in Greece about Augustus' (and his successors') preference of the "West" (partly on the grounds of Augustus' dissociation from the expressly "philhellene" policies of Mark Antony). More than any other Roman ruler, Nero had flattered the Greeks, many of whom preferred to repress reality through nostalgic feelings about past political and cultural greatness. The odd and embarrassing aspects of Nero's travels to Greece were ultimately excused through his granting of "freedom" for Greece. The collective memory made the liberation more attractive than it actually was due to the fact that Vespasian rescinded it at the first best opportunity. Learned men such as Plutarch and Pausanias compared Nero's good deeds for Greece with his errors. To that extent, Nero's continued policies toward the East might have had some useful outcomes, despite all their peculiarities.

There is a discrepancy between modern judgments and contemporary perceptions also regarding the behavior of the Parthians toward Nero. The Parthians definitely did not appraise the outcome of the battles for Armenia as signs of the empire's weakness. They were satisfied with what was accomplished and held Nero to be the progenitor of a policy of balance. King Vologaeses is said to have requested that the memory of the deceased princeps be honored. The notion of the Parthian kings having sentimental leanings as it were for Nero and his policies – according to which Tiridates would have spoken favorably about his Roman sojourn – is confirmed by news of another "false" Nero who incorporated Parthian support for Nero's return into his plans.

The undertaking of the otherwise unknown Terentius Maximus, similar to the situation with the "false" Nero in 69, was facilitated by virtue of certain artistic abilities and physical resemblance, which, ten years after the disappearance of the princeps, was no longer all that difficult to feign. His popularity in Asia Minor was evidently not insignificant. Terentius Maximus attempted to instrumentalize a conflict between the Parthian Artabanos and Titus regarding the continuation of his plans. He was successful for a short time but then handed over to the Romans.

Such swindling endeavors did not hurt the popularity of the "philhellene" princeps, which was widespread in the East. Some who were dissatisfied with present conditions spoke of the return of the emperor in the first decades after Nero's death, when it was still biographically feasible. At the time of his "disappearance" Nero was only thirty-two years old. According to Dio Chrysostom in a speech he wrote around the turn of the century, "for so far as the rest of his subjects were concerned, there was nothing to prevent his continuing to be Emperor for all time, seeing that even now everybody wishes he were still alive. And the great majority do believe that he is, although in a certain sense he has died not once but often, along with those who had been firmly convinced that he was still alive" (*Discourse* 21.10).

In another way the Jews also had an interest in Nero's "return." They did not want to reestablish the ancient glory; quite the contrary, they wanted to avenge Vespasian and Titus for destroying the Jewish polity. In a Jewish prophecy Terentius Maximus became the man who would travel across the Euphrates from Parthia to punish Rome in armed struggle.

Christian notions of a "return" of Nero served other purposes. Despite the surprisingly delayed Christian writings about Nero as a persecutor of Christians, his image in Christian communities might have been similar to how he was perceived by Jews. The tradition of the martyrdom of the Apostles Peter and Paul in the context of Neronian persecution became widespread in the late first century at the latest and have made this a lasting image. The beast in Revelation (13.1) might even be an image of Nero who will return to destroy Rome. For Christian authors of the late

Figure 9   Peter Ustinov as Nero (*Quo Vadis*, 1951). MGM/
The Kobal Collection

antiquity, Nero the arsonist and persecutor of Christians
became the incarnation of the anti-Christ who will come
to the Last Judgment. Memories of Nero's popularity among
the people of the city of Rome nevertheless were not totally lost. In addition to undisputed rulers such as Trajan,
Nero – surprisingly enough – also appears on bronze coins,
so-called contorniate medallions. Recollections of the circus games are emphasized, aiming to bring forth memories

of this aspect of Nero's rule, perhaps in deliberate opposition to Christian rulers of the fourth and fifth centuries.

Outside the circle of people interested in history, memories of Nero are often reduced even in modern times to the great fire of Rome and Nero's role in the persecution of Christians. The image of Nero in the twentieth century was greatly influenced by one of the greatest bestsellers of all time: *Quo Vadis*, first published in 1896. The Polish author Henryk Sienkiewicz received the 1905 Nobel Prize for Literature for the novel. This book depicts Nero solely from the perspective of his role in Christian persecution, although definitely more as an overwhelmed dilettante than as a "main character" of the time. This literary portrait of Nero was then reinforced when the book was filmed in 1954. Only very few people who are interested in the history of Nero will not have a lyre-playing Peter Ustinov in their mind's eye.

The marketing specialists in the computer industry are no exception. There is software to "burn" CD-ROMs that carries the tradition-conscious name "NERO BURNING ROM."

Appendix

Suetonius: The Lives of the
Twelve Caesars: An English
Translation, Augmented with the
Biographies of Contemporary
Statesmen, Orators, Poets, and
Other Associates. Nero (extracts).
Publishing Editor. J. Eugene Reed.
Alexander Thomson. Philadelphia.
Gebbie & Co. 1889.

I. Two celebrated families, the Calvini and Ahenobarbi,
sprang from the race of the Domitii. The Ahenobarbi de-
rive both their extraction and their cognomen from one
Lucius Domitius, of whom we have this tradition: As he
was returning out of the country to Rome, he was met by
two young men of a most august appearance, who desired
him to announce to the Senate and people a victory, of
which no certain intelligence had yet reached the city. To
prove that they were more than mortals, they stroked his
cheeks, and thus changed his hair, which was black, to a
bright color, resembling that of brass; this mark of distinction descended to his posterity, for they had generally red
beards. This family had the honor of seven consulships,
one triumph, and two censorships; and being admitted into

the patrician order, they continued the use of the same cognomen, with no other praenomina than those of Gnaeus and Lucius. These, however, they assumed with singular irregularity; three persons in succession sometimes adhering to one of them, and then they were changed alternately. For the first, second, and third of the Ahenobarbi had the praenomen of Lucius, and again the three following, successively, that of Gnaeus, while those who came after were called, by turns, one, Lucius, and the other, Gnaeus. It appears to me proper to give a short account of several of the family, to show that Nero so far degenerated from the noble qualities of his ancestors that he retained only their vices, as if those alone had been transmitted to him by his descent.

II. To begin, therefore, at a remote period, his great-grandfather's grandfather, Gnaeus Domitius, when he was tribune of the people, being offended with the high priests for electing another than himself in the place of his father, obtained the transfer of the right of election from the colleges of the priests to the people. In his consulship, having conquered the Allobroges and the Arverni, he made a progress through the province, mounted upon an elephant, with a body of soldiers attending him, in a sort of triumphal pomp. Of this person the orator Licinius Crassus said, "It was no wonder he had a brazen beard, who had a face of iron, and a heart of lead." His son, during his praetorship, proposed that Cneius Caesar, upon the expiration of his consulship, should be called to account before the Senate for his administration of that office, which was supposed to be contrary both to the omens and the laws. Afterwards, when he was consul himself, he tried to deprive Cneius of the command of the army, and having been, by intrigue and cabal, appointed his successor, he was made prisoner at Corfinium, in the beginning of the civil war. Being set at liberty, he went to Marseilles, which was then besieged; where, having by his presence animated the people to hold out, he suddenly deserted them, and at last was slain in the battle of Pharsalia. He was a man of little constancy, and of a sullen temper. In despair of his fortunes, he had recourse to poison, but was so terrified at the thoughts of death that, immediately repenting, he vomited it up again, and gave freedom to his physician for having, with great prudence and wisdom, given him only a gentle dose of the poison. When Cneius Pompey was consulting with his friends in what manner he should conduct himself toward those who were neuter and took no part in the contest, he was the only one who proposed that they should be treated as enemies.

III.   He left a son who was, without doubt, the best of the family. By the Pedian law, he was condemned, although innocent, amongst others who were concerned in the death of Caesar. Upon this, he went over to Brutus and Cassius, his near relations; and, after their death, not only kept together the fleet, the command of which had been given him some time before, but even increased it.

At last, when the party had everywhere been defeated, he voluntarily surrendered it to Mark Antony, considering it a service for which the latter owed him no small obligations. Of all those who were condemned by the law above-mentioned, he was the only man who was restored to his country, and filled the highest offices. When the civil war again broke out, he was appointed lieutenant under the same Antony, and offered the chief command by those who were ashamed of Cleopatra; but not daring, on account of a sudden indisposition with which he was seized, either to accept or refuse it, he went over to Augustus, and died a few days after, not without an aspersion cast upon his memory. For Antony gave out that he was induced to change sides by his impatience to be with his mistress, Servilia Nais.

IV.   This Gnaeus had a son, named Domitius, who was later well known as the nominal purchaser of the family property left by Augustus' will, and no less famous in his youth for his dexterity in chariot-driving than he was later for the triumphal ornaments which he obtained in the German war. But he was a man of great arrogance, prodigality, and cruelty. When he was aedile, he obliged Lucius Plancus, the censor, to give him the way; and in his praetorship, and consulship, he made Roman knights and married women act on the stage. He gave hunts of wild beasts, both in the Circus and in all the wards of the city, and also a show of gladiators, but with such barbarity that Augustus, after privately reprimanding him, to no purpose, was obliged to restrain him by a public edict.

V. By the elder Antonia he had Nero's father, a man of execrable character in every part of his life. During his attendance upon Caius Caesar in the East, he killed a freedman of his own, for refusing to drink as much as he ordered him. Being dismissed for this from Caesar's society, he did not mend his habits, for, in a village upon the Appian road, he suddenly whipped his horses and drove his chariot, on purpose, over a poor boy, crushing him to pieces. At Rome, he struck out the eye of a Roman knight in the Forum, just because of some free language in a dispute between them. He was likewise so fraudulent that he not only cheated some silversmiths of the price of goods he had bought from them, but, during his praetorship, defrauded the owners of chariots in the Circensian games of the prizes due to them for their victory. When his sister jeered at him after the complaints made by the leaders of the several parties, he agreed to sanction a law, "That, for the future, the prizes should be immediately paid." A little before the death of Tiberius, he was prosecuted for treason, adulteries, and incest with his sister Lepida, but escaped in the timely change of affairs, and died of a dropsy at Pyrgi, leaving behind him his son, Nero, whom he had by Agrippina, the daughter of Germanicus.

VI. Nero was born at Antium, nine months after the death of Tiberius, upon the eighteenth of the calends of

January [December 15], just as the sun rose, so that its beams touched him before they could well reach the earth. While many fearful conjectures in respect to his future fortune were formed by different persons from the circumstances of his nativity, a saying of his father, Domitius, was regarded as an ill presage, who told his friends who were congratulating him upon the occasion, "That nothing but what was detestable and pernicious to the public could ever be produced of him and Agrippina." Another manifest prognostic of his future infelicity occurred upon his lustration day. Caius Caesar, requested by his sister to give the child a name he thought proper, looked at his uncle, Claudius, who afterwards, when emperor, adopted Nero, and gave his name: not seriously, but only in jest, with Agrippina treating it with contempt, because Claudius at that time was a mere laughing-stock at the palace. He lost his father when he was three years old, and was heir to a third part of his estate, of which he never got possession, the whole being seized by his co-heir, Caius. His mother was banished soon after, and he lived with his aunt Lepida in a very necessitous condition, under the care of two tutors, a dancing-master and a barber. After Claudius came to the empire, he not only recovered his father's estate, but was enriched with the additional inheritance of that of his stepfather, Crispus Passienus. Upon his mother's recall from banishment, he was advanced to such favor, through Nero's powerful interest with the emperor, that, it was reported, assassins were employed by Messalina, Claudius' wife, to strangle him, as Britannicus' rival, while he was taking his noonday repose. In addition to the story, it was said that they were frightened by a serpent, which crept from under his cushion and ran away. The tale was occasioned by finding on his couch, near the pillow, the skin of a snake, which, by his mother's order, he wore for some time upon his right arm, enclosed in a bracelet of gold. This amulet he eventually laid aside, from aversion to her memory; but he sought for it again in vain, in the time of his extremity.

VII. When he was yet a mere boy, before he arrived at the age of puberty, during the celebration of the Circensian games, he performed his part in the Trojan play with a degree of firmness which gained him great applause. In his eleventh year he was adopted by Claudius, and placed under the tuition of Annaeus Seneca, who had been made a senator. It is said that Seneca dreamt, the night after, that he was giving a lesson to Caius Caesar. Nero soon verified his dream, betraying the cruelty of his disposition in every way he could. For he attempted to persuade his father that his brother, Britannicus, was nothing but a changeling, because the latter had saluted him, notwithstanding his adoption, by the name of Ahenobarbus, as usual. When his aunt, Lepida, was brought to trial, he appeared in court as a witness against her, to gratify his mother, who persecuted the accused. On his introduction into the Forum, at the age of manhood, he gave a largess to the people and a donative to the soldiers; for the praetorian cohorts, he appointed a solemn procession under arms, and marched at the head of them with a shield in his hand; after which he went to return thanks to his father in the Senate. Before Claudius, likewise, at the time he was consul, he made a speech for the Bolognese, in Latin, and for the Rhodians and people of Ilium, in Greek. He had the jurisdiction of praefect of the city, for the first time, during the Latin festival, during which the most celebrated advocates brought before him, not short and trifling causes, as is usual in that case, but trials of importance, notwithstanding they had instructions from Claudius himself to the contrary. Soon afterwards, he married Octavia, and exhibited the Circensian games, and hunting of wild beasts, in honor of Claudius.

VIII. He was seventeen years of age at the death of that prince, and as soon as that event was made public, he went out to the cohort on guard between the hours of six and seven, for the omens were so disastrous that no earlier time of the day was judged proper. On the steps before the palace gate, he was unanimously saluted by the soldiers as their emperor, and then carried in a litter to the camp; thence, after making a short speech to the troops, into the senate-house, where he continued until the evening; of all the immense honors which were heaped upon him, he refused none but the title of "father of the fatherland," on account of his youth.

IX.   He began his reign with a show of dutiful regard to the memory of Claudius, whom he buried with the utmost pomp and magnificence, pronouncing the funeral oration himself, and then had him enrolled amongst the gods. He paid likewise the highest honors to the memory of his father Domitius. He left the management of affairs, both public and private, to his mother. The word which he gave on the first day of his reign to the tribune on guard was "The Best of Mothers," and afterwards he frequently appeared with her in the streets of Rome in her litter. He settled a colony at Antium, in which he placed the veteran soldiers belonging to the guards, and obliged several of the richest centurions of the first rank to transfer their residence there, where he likewise made a noble harbor at prodigious expense.

X.   To establish still further his character, he declared "that he designed to govern according to the model of Augustus," and omitted no opportunity of showing his generosity, clemency, and complaisance. The more burthensome taxes he either entirely abolished, or diminished. He reduced the rewards appointed for informers by the Papian law to a quarter, and distributed to the people four hundred sesterces per man. To the noblest of the senators who were much reduced in their circumstances, he granted annual allowances, in some cases as much as five hundred thousand sesterces; and to the praetorian cohorts a monthly allowance of corn gratis. When called upon to subscribe the sentence, according to custom, of a criminal condemned to die, he said, "I wish I had never learned to read and write." He continually saluted people of the several orders by name, without a prompter. When the Senate returned him their thanks for his good government, he replied, "It will be time enough to do so when I shall have deserved it." He admitted the common people to see him perform his exercises in the Campus Martius. He frequently declaimed in public, and recited verses of his own composing, not only at home but in the theater, so much to the joy of all the people that public prayers were appointed to be put to the gods upon that account; and the verses which had been publicly read were, after being written in gold letters, consecrated to Jupiter Capitolinus.

XI. He presented the people with a great number and variety of spectacles, such as the Juvenal and Circensian games, stage-plays, and an exhibition of gladiators. In the Juvenal, he even admitted senators and aged matrons to perform parts. In the Circensian games, he assigned the equestrian order seats apart from the rest of the people, and had races performed by chariots each drawn by four camels. In the games which he instituted for the eternal duration of the empire, and therefore ordered to be called *Maximi*, many of the senatorian and equestrian order, of both sexes, performed. A distinguished Roman knight descended on the stage by a rope, mounted on an elephant. A Roman play, likewise, composed by Afranius, was brought to the stage. It was entitled "The Fire," and in it the performers were allowed to carry off, and to keep for themselves, the furniture of the house, which, as the plot of the play required, was burned down in the theater. Every day during the solemnity, many thousand articles of all descriptions were thrown amongst the people to scramble for; such as fowls of different kinds, tickets for corn, clothes, gold, silver, gems, pearls, pictures, slaves, beasts of burden, wild beasts that had been tamed; at last, ships, lots of houses, and lands, were offered as prizes in a lottery.

XII.   These games he beheld from the front of the pro-
scenium. In the show of gladiators, which he exhibited in a
wooden amphitheater, built within a year in the district of
the Campus Martius, he ordered that none should be slain,
not even the condemned criminals employed in the com-
bats. He secured four hundred senators, and six hundred
Roman knights, amongst whom were some of unbroken
fortunes and unblemished reputation, to act as gladiators.
From the same orders, he engaged persons to encounter
wild beasts, and for various other services in the theater.
He presented the public with the representation of a naval
fight, upon sea-water, with huge fishes swimming in it;
and also the Pyrrhic dance, performed by certain youths, to
each of whom, after the performance was over, he granted
the freedom of Rome. During this diversion, a bull covered
Pasiphaë, concealed within a wooden statue of a cow, as
many of the spectators believed. Icarus, upon his first
attempt to fly, fell on the stage close to the emperor's
pavilion, and bespattered him with blood. For he very
seldom presided in the games, but used to view them re-
clining on a couch, at first through some narrow apertures,
but afterwards with the *Podium* quite open. He was the
first who instituted, in imitation of the Greeks, a trial of
skill in the three several exercises of music, wrestling, and
horse-racing, to be performed at Rome every five years, and
which he called Neronia. Upon the dedication of his bath
and gymnasium, he furnished the senate and the equestrian order with oil. He appointed as judges of the trial
men of consular rank, chosen by lot, who sat with the
praetors. At this time he went down into the orchestra
among the senators, and received the crown for the best
performance in Latin prose and verse, for which several
persons of the greatest merit contended, but they unanimously yielded to him. The crown for the best performer
on the harp was likewise awarded to him by the judges; he
devoutly saluted it, and ordered it to be carried to the statue
of Augustus. In the gymnastic exercises, which he presented in the Septa, while they were preparing the great

sacrifice of an ox, he shaved his beard for the first time, and, putting it up in a casket of gold studded with pearls of great price, consecrated it to Jupiter Capitolinus. He invited the vestal virgins to see the wrestlers perform, because, at Olympia, the priestesses of Ceres are allowed the privilege of witnessing that exhibition.

XIII. Amongst the spectacles presented by him, the solemn entrance of Tiridates into the city deserves to be mentioned. This personage, who was king of Armenia, he invited to Rome with very liberal promises. But being prevented by very unfavorable weather from showing him to the people upon the day fixed by proclamation, he took the first opportunity which occurred; several cohorts were drawn up under arms, about the temples and in the Forum, while he was seated on a curule chair on the rostra, in a triumphal dress, amidst the military standards and ensigns. Upon Tiridates advancing toward him, on a stage made shelving for the purpose, he permitted him to throw himself at his feet, but quickly raised him with his right hand, and kissed him. The emperor then, at the king's request, took the turban from his head and replaced it by a crown, while a person of praetorian rank proclaimed in Latin the words in which the prince addressed the emperor as a suppliant. After this ceremony, the king was conducted to the theater where, after renewing his obeisance, Nero seated him on his right hand. Being then greeted by universal acclamation with the title of Emperor, and sending his laurel crown to the Capitol, Nero shut the temple of the two-faced Janus, as though there now existed no war throughout the Roman empire.

XIV. He filled the consulship four times: the first for two months, the second and last for six, and the third for four; the two intermediate ones he held successively, but the others after an interval of some years between them.

XV. In the administration of justice, he scarcely ever gave his decision on the pleadings before the next day, and then in writing. His manner of hearing causes was not to allow any adjournment, but to dispatch them in order as they stood. When he withdrew to consult his assessors, he did not debate the matter openly with them; but after silently and privately reading over their opinions, which they gave separately in writing, he pronounced sentence from the tribunal according to his own view of the case, as if it was the opinion of the majority. For a long time he would not admit the sons of freedmen into the Senate; and those who had been admitted by former princes, he excluded from all public offices. To supernumerary candidates he gave command in the legions, to comfort them under the delay of their hopes. The consulship he commonly conferred for six months, and when one of the two consuls died a little before the first of January, he substituted no one in his place, as he disliked what had been formerly done for Caninius Rebilus on such an occasion, who was consul for one day only. He allowed triumphal honors only to those who were of quaestorian rank, and to some of the equestrian order, and bestowed them without regard to military service. And instead of the quaestors, whose office it properly was, he frequently ordered that the addresses, which he sent to the Senate on certain occasions, should be read by the consuls.

XVI. He devised a new style of building in the city, ordering piazzas to be erected before all houses both in the streets and detached, to give facilities from their terraces, in case of fire, for preventing it from spreading; and these he built at his own expense. He likewise designed to extend the city walls as far as Ostia, and bring the sea from thence by a canal into the old city. Many severe regulations and new orders were made in his time. A sumptuary law was enacted. Public suppers were limited to the Sportulae, and victualling-houses restrained from selling any dressed victuals, except pulses and herbs, whereas before they sold all kinds of meat. He likewise inflicted punishments on the Christians, a sort of people who held a new and impious superstition. He forbade the revels of the charioteers, who had long assumed a license to stroll about, and established for themselves a kind of prescriptive right to cheat and thieve, making a jest of it. The partisans of the rival theatrical performers were banished, as well as the actors themselves.

XVII. To prevent forgery, a method was then first invented of having writings bored, run through three times with a thread, and then sealed. It was likewise provided that in wills, the two first pages, with only the testator's name upon them, should be presented blank to those who were to sign them as witnesses; and that no one who wrote a will for another should insert any legacy for himself. It was likewise ordained that clients should pay their advocates a certain reasonable fee, but nothing for the court, which was to be gratuitous, the charges for it being paid out of the public treasury; that causes, the cognizance of which had hitherto belonged to the judges of the exchequer, should be transferred to the forum, and the ordinary tribunals; and that all appeals from the judges should be made to the Senate.

XVIII. He never entertained the least ambition or hope of augmenting and extending the frontiers of the empire. On the contrary, he had thoughts of withdrawing the troops from Britain, and was only restrained from so doing by the fear of appearing to detract from the glory of his father. All that he did was to reduce the kingdom of Pontus, which was ceded to him by Polemon, and also the Alps, upon the death of Cottius, to the form of a province.

XIX. He undertook foreign expeditions only twice, one to Alexandria and the other to Achaea, but he abandoned the prosecution of the former on the very day fixed for his departure, being deterred both by ill omens and by the hazards of the voyage. For while he was making the circuit of the temples, having seated himself in that of Vesta, when he attempted to rise, the skirt of his robe stuck fast, and he was instantly seized with such a dimness in his eyes that he could not see a yard in front of him. In Achaea, he attempted to make a cut through the isthmus; and, having made a speech encouraging his praetorians to set about the work, on a signal given by the sound of a trumpet he first broke ground with a spade, and carried off a basket full of earth upon his shoulders. He made preparations for an expedition to the Pass of the Caspian mountains, forming a new legion out of his late levies in Italy, of men all six feet tall, which he called the phalanx of Alexander the Great. These transactions, in part unexceptionable, and in part highly commendable, I have brought into one view, in order to separate them from the scandalous and criminal part of his conduct, of which I shall now give an account.

XX. Among the other liberal arts which he was taught in his youth, he was instructed in music, and immediately after his advancement to the empire, he sent for Terpnus, a harpist, who flourished at that time with the highest reputation. Sitting with him for several days as he sang and played after supper until late at night, he began by degrees to practice the instrument himself. Nor did he omit any of those expedients which artists in music adopt for the preservation and improvement of their voices. He would lie on his back with a sheet of lead upon his breast, clear his stomach and bowels by vomits and clysters, and forbear the eating of fruits, or food prejudicial to the voice. Encouraged by his proficiency, though his voice was neither loud nor clear, he was desirous of appearing on the stage, frequently repeating amongst his friends a Greek proverb to this effect: "that no one had any regard for music which they never heard." Accordingly, he made his first public appearance at Naples, and although the theater quivered with the sudden shock of an earthquake, he did not desist until he had finished the piece of music he had begun. He played and sang in the same place several times, and for several days together, only now and then taking a little respite to refresh his voice. Impatient of retirement, it was his custom to go from the bath to the theater; and after dining in the orchestra, amidst a crowded assembly of the people, he promised them in Greek, "that after he had drunk a little, he would give them a tune which would make their ears tingle." Being highly pleased with the songs that were sung in his praise by some Alexandrians belonging to the fleet which had just arrived at Naples, he sent for more of these singers from Alexandria. At the same time, he chose young men of the equestrian order and more than five thousand robust young fellows from the common people to learn various kinds of applause, called *bombi*, *imbrices*, and *testae*, which they were to practice in his favor whenever he performed. They were divided into several parties, were remarkable for their fine heads of hair, and were extremely well dressed, with rings on their left hands. The leaders of these bands were given salaries of forty thousand sesterces.

XXI. At Rome also, being extremely proud of his singing, he ordered the games called Neronia to be celebrated before the time fixed for their return. All now becoming importunate to hear "his heavenly voice," he informed them "that he would gratify those who desired it at the gardens." But as the soldiers then on guard seconded the voice of the people, he promised to comply with their request immediately, and with all his heart. He instantly ordered his name to be added to the list of musicians who proposed to contend, and having thrown his lot into the urn among the rest, took his turn; he entered, attended by the prefects of the praetorian cohorts bearing his harp, and followed by the military tribunes and several of his intimate friends. After he had taken his station and made the usual prelude, he commanded Cluvius Rufus, a man of consular rank, to proclaim in the theater that he intended to sing the story of Niobe. This he accordingly did, and continued it until nearly ten o'clock, but deferred the disposal of the crown, and the remaining part of the solemnity, until the next year, that he might have more frequent opportunities of performing. But that being too long, he could not refrain from often appearing as a public performer during the interval. He made no scruple of exhibiting on the stage, even in the spectacles presented to the people by private persons, and was offered, by one of the praetors, no less than a million sesterces for his services. He likewise sang tragedies in a mask; the visors of the heroes and gods, and also of the heroines and goddesses, were formed into a resemblance of his own face, and that of any woman he was in love with. Amongst the rest, he sang *Canace in Labour*, *Orestes the Murderer of his Mother*, *Oedipus Blinded*, and *Hercules Mad*. In the last tragedy, it is said that a young sentinel posted at the entrance of the stage, seeing him in a prison dress and bound with fetters, as the fable of the play required, ran to his assistance.

XXII.   He had from childhood an extravagant passion for horses, and his constant talk was of the Circensian races, notwithstanding it was prohibited him. Lamenting once, among his fellow-pupils, the case of a charioteer of the green party, who was dragged round the circus at the tail of his chariot and reprimanded by his tutor for it, he pretended that he was talking of Hector. In the beginning of his reign, he used to amuse himself daily with chariots drawn by four horses, made of ivory, on a table. He attended all the lesser exhibitions in the circus, at first privately, but later openly, so that nobody ever doubted his presence on any particular day. Nor did he conceal his desire to have the number of prizes doubled; as the races were increased accordingly, the diversion continued until a late hour, the leaders of parties refusing now to bring out their companies for any time less than the whole day. Upon this, he took a fancy for driving the chariot himself, and did so even in public. Having made his first experiment in the gardens, amidst crowds of slaves and other rabble, he at length performed in the view of all the people, in the Circus Maximus, while one of his freedmen dropped the napkin in the place where the magistrates used to give the signal. Not satisfied with exhibiting various specimens of his skill in those arts at Rome, he went over to Achaea, as has already been said, principally for this purpose. The several cities in which solemn trials of musical skill used to be publicly held had resolved to send him the crowns belonging to those who bore away the prize. These he accepted so graciously that he not only gave the deputies who brought them an immediate audience, but even invited them to his table. Being requested by some of them to sing at supper, and prodigiously applauded, he said, "the Greeks were the only people who had an ear for music, and were the only good judges of him and his attainments." Without delay he commenced his journey and, on his arrival at Cassiope, exhibited his first musical performance before the altar of Jupiter Cassius.

XXIII. He later appeared at the celebration of all public games in Greece: those that fell in different years he brought within the compass of one, and some he ordered to be celebrated a second time in the same year. At Olympia, likewise, contrary to custom, he appointed a public performance of music: and so that he might meet with no interruption in this employment, when he was informed by his freedman Helius that affairs at Rome required his presence, he wrote to him with these words: "Though now all your hopes and wishes are for my speedy return, yet you ought rather to advise and hope that I may come back with a character worthy of Nero." During his musical performance, nobody was allowed to stir out of the theater on any account, however necessary; it is said that some women with child were delivered there. Many of the spectators, who were quite wearied with hearing and applauding him, slipped privately over the walls, because the town gates were shut, or pretended to be dead and were carried out for their funeral. With what extreme anxiety he engaged in these contests, with what keen desire to bear away the prize, and with how much awe of the judges is scarcely to be believed. If his adversaries were on a level with himself he would watch them narrowly, defame them privately, and sometimes, upon meeting them, rail at them in very scurrilous language; or bribe them, if they were better performers than himself. He always addressed the judges with the most profound reverence before he began, telling them that "he had done all things that were necessary, by way of preparation, but that the issue of the approaching trial was in the hand of fortune; and that they, as wise and skillful men, ought to exclude from their judgment things merely accidental." Upon their encouraging him to have a good heart, he went off with more assurance, but not entirely free from anxiety; he interpreted the silence and modesty of some of them as sourness and ill-nature, and said that he was suspicious of them.

XXIV. In these contests, he adhered so strictly to the rules that he never dared spit, nor wipe the sweat from his forehead in any other way than with his sleeve. Having, in the performance of a tragedy, dropped his scepter, and not quickly recovering it, he was in a great fright lest he should be set aside for the miscarriage, and could not regain his assurance until an actor who stood by swore he was certain it had not been observed in the midst of the acclamations and exultations of the people. When the prize was adjudged to him, he always proclaimed it himself, and even entered the list with the heralds. In order that no memory nor the least monument might remain of any other victor in the sacred Grecian games, he ordered all their statues and pictures to be pulled down, dragged away with hooks, and thrown into the common sewers. He drove the chariot with various numbers of horses, and at the Olympic games with no fewer than ten; though, in a poem of his, he had reflected upon Mithridates for that innovation. When he was thrown out of his chariot, he was put back into it, but could not retain his seat and was obliged to give it up before he reached the goal, but was crowned notwithstanding. On his departure he declared the whole province a free country, and conferred upon the judges in the several games the freedom of Rome, with large sums of money. All these favors he proclaimed himself with his own voice, from the middle of the *Stadium*, during the solemnity of the Isthmian games.

XXV.   On his return from Greece, arriving at Naples, because he had commenced his career as a public performer in that city, he made his entrance in a chariot drawn by white horses through a breach in the city-wall, according to the practice of those who were victorious in the sacred Grecian games. In the same manner he entered Antium, Alba, and Rome. He made his entry into the city riding in the same chariot in which Augustus had triumphed, in a purple tunic and a cloak embroidered with golden stars, on his head the crown won at Olympia, and in his right hand that which was given him at the Parthian games: the rest were carried in a procession before him, with inscriptions denoting the places where they had been won, from whom, and in what plays or musical performances, while a train followed him with loud acclamations, crying out that "they were the emperor's attendants, and the soldiers of his triumph." Having then caused an arch of the Circus Maximus to be taken down, he passed through the breach, and also through the Velabrum and the Forum, to the Palatine hill and the temple of Apollo. Everywhere, as he marched along, victims were slain, while the streets were strewn with saffron, and birds, chaplets, and sweetmeats scattered abroad. He suspended the sacred crowns in his chamber, about his beds; he caused statues of himself to be erected in the attire of a harpist, and had his likeness stamped upon the coin in the same dress. After this period, he was so far from abating anything of his application to music that, for the preservation of his voice, he never addressed the soldiers except by messages, or with some person to deliver his speeches for him, when he thought fit to make his appearance amongst them. Nor did he ever do anything, either in jest or in earnest, without a voice-master standing by him to caution him against overstraining his vocal organs, and to apply a handkerchief to his mouth when he did. He offered his friendship, or avowed open enmity, to many, according to whether they were lavish or sparing in giving him their applause.

XXVI.   Petulance, lewdness, luxury, avarice, and cruelty he practiced at first with reserve and in private, as if prompted to them only by the folly of youth, but, even then, the world was of the opinion that they were the faults of his nature, and not of his age. After it was dark, he used to enter the taverns disguised in a cap or a wig, and ramble about the streets in sport, which was not void of mischief. He used to beat those he met coming home from supper; and, if they made any resistance, would wound them, and throw them into the common sewer. He broke open and robbed shops, establishing an auction at home for selling his booty. In the scuffles which took place on those occasions, he often ran the hazard of losing his eyes, and even his life – he was beaten almost to death by a senator for handling his wife indecently. After this adventure, he never again ventured abroad at that time of night without some tribunes following him at a little distance. In the daytime he would be carried to the theater incognito in a litter, placing himself upon the upper part of the pro-scenium, where he not only witnessed the quarrels which arose on account of the performances, but also encouraged them. When they came to blows, and stones and pieces of broken benches began to fly about, he threw them plenti-fully amongst the people, and once even broke a praetor's head.

XXVII.   His vices gaining strength by degrees, he laid aside his jocular amusements and all disguise, breaking out into enormous crimes without the least attempt to conceal them. His revels were prolonged from midday to midnight, while he was frequently refreshed by warm baths, and, in the summer time, by such as were cooled with snow. He often supped in public, in the Naumachia, with the sluices shut, or in the Campus Martius or the Circus Maximus, waited upon at table by common prostitutes of the town and Syrian strumpets and gleegirls. As often as he went down the Tiber to Ostia, or coasted through the gulf of Baiae, booths furnished as brothels and eating-houses were erected along the shore and river banks, before which stood matrons who, like bawds and hostesses, allured him to land. It was also his custom to invite himself to supper with his friends, at one of which was expended no less than four million sesterces in chaplets, and at another something more in roses.

XXVIII. Besides the abuse of free-born boys and the debauch of married women, he committed a rape upon Rubria, a vestal virgin. He was upon the point of marrying Acte, his freedwoman, having suborned some men of consular rank to swear that she was of royal descent. He gelded the boy Sporus, and endeavored to transform him into a woman. He even went so far as to marry him, with all the usual formalities of a marriage settlement, the rose-colored nuptial veil, and a numerous company at the wedding. When the ceremony was over, he had him conducted like a bride to his own house, and treated him as his wife. It was jocularly observed by some person, "that it would have been well for mankind, had such a wife fallen to the lot of his father Domitius." This Sporus he carried about with him in a litter round the solemn assemblies and fairs of Greece, and afterwards at Rome through the Sigillaria, dressed in the rich attire of an empress, kissing him from time to time as they rode together. That he entertained an incestuous passion for his mother, but was deterred by her enemies, for fear that this haughty and overbearing woman should, by her compliance, get him entirely into her power and govern in everything, was universally believed, especially after he had introduced amongst his concubines a strumpet who was reported to have a strong resemblance to Agrippina.

* * *

XXIX.   He prostituted his own chastity to such a degree that after he had defiled every part of his person with some unnatural pollution, he at last invented an extraordinary kind of diversion: to be let out of a den in the arena, covered with the skin of a wild beast, and then assail with violence the private parts of both men and women, while they were bound to stakes. After he had vented his furious passion upon them, he finished the play in the embraces of his freedman Doryphorus, to whom he was married in the same way that Sporus had been married to himself, imitating the cries and shrieks of young virgins when they are ravished. I have been informed from numerous sources that he firmly believed no man in the world would be chaste, or any part of his person undefiled, but that most men concealed that vice, and were cunning enough to keep it secret. To those, therefore, who frankly owned their unnatural lewdness, he forgave all other crimes.

XXX.   He thought there was no other use of riches and money than to squander them away profusely, regarding all those who kept their expenses within due bounds as sordid wretches and extolling those who lavished away and wasted all they possessed as truly noble and generous souls. He praised and admired his uncle Caius upon no account more than for squandering in a short time the vast treasure left him by Tiberius. Accordingly, he was himself extravagant and profuse, beyond all bounds. He spent upon Tiridates eight hundred thousand sesterces a day, a sum almost incredible, and, at his departure, presented him with upwards of a million. He likewise bestowed upon Menecrates, the harpist, and Spicillus, a gladiator, the estates and houses of men who had received the honor of a triumph. He enriched the usurer Cercopithecus Panerotes with estates both in town and country, and gave him a funeral which was in pomp and magnificence little inferior to that of princes. He never wore the same garment twice.

He has been known to stake four hundred thousand sesterces on a throw of the dice. It was his custom to fish with a golden net, drawn by silken cords of purple and scarlet. It is said that he never traveled with less than a thousand baggage-carts; the mules were all shod with silver, and the drivers dressed in scarlet jackets of the finest Canusian cloth, with a numerous train of footmen, and troops of Mazacans, with bracelets on their arms, and mounted upon horses in splendid trappings.

XXXI.   In nothing was he more prodigal than in his buildings. He completed his palace by continuing it from the Palatine to the Esquiline hill, calling the building at first only "The Passage," but after it was burnt down and rebuilt, "The Golden House." Of its dimensions and furniture, it may be sufficient to say thus much: the porch was so high that there stood in it a colossal statue of himself a hundred and twenty feet in height; and the space included in it was so ample that it had triple porticos a mile in length, and a lake like a sea, surrounded with buildings which had the appearance of a city. Within its area were corn fields, vineyards, pastures, and woods, containing a vast number of animals of various kinds, both wild and tame. In other parts it was entirely overlaid with gold, and adorned with jewels and mother-of-pearl. The supper rooms were vaulted, and compartments of the ceilings, inlaid with ivory, were made to revolve, and scatter flowers; they also contained pipes which shed unguents upon the guests. The chief banqueting room was circular, and revolved perpetually, night and day, in imitation of the motion of the celestial bodies. The baths were supplied with water from the sea and the Albula. Upon the dedication of this magnificent house after it was finished, all he said in approval of it was, "that he had now a dwelling fit for a man." He commenced making a pond for the reception of all the hot springs from Baiae, which he designed to have continued from Misenum to the Avernian lake, in a conduit, enclosed in galleries: and also a canal from Avernum to Ostia, that ships might pass from one to the other without a sea voyage. The length of the proposed canal was one hundred and sixty miles; and it was intended to be of breadth sufficient to permit ships with five banks of oars to pass each other. For the execution of these designs, he ordered all prisoners, in every part of the empire, to be brought to Italy; and that even those who were convicted of the most heinous crimes, in lieu of any other sentence, should be condemned to work at them. He was encouraged to all this wild and enormous profusion, not only by the great revenue of the empire, but by the sudden hopes given him of an immense hidden treasure, which queen Dido, upon her flight from Tyre, had brought with her to Africa. This, a Roman knight pretended to assure him, upon good grounds, was still hidden there in some deep caverns, and might with a little labor be recovered.

XXXII.   But being disappointed in his expectations of this resource, and reduced to such difficulties for want of money that he was obliged to defer paying his troops and the rewards due to the veterans, he resolved upon supplying his necessities by means of false accusations and plunder. In the first place, he ordered that if any freedman, without sufficient reason, bore the name of the family to which he belonged, half instead of three-fourths of his estate should be brought into the exchequer at his decease; also that the estates of all such persons as had not in their wills been mindful of their prince should be confiscated; and that the lawyers who had drawn or dictated such wills should be liable to a fine. He ordained likewise that all words and actions upon which any informer could ground a prosecution should be deemed treason. He demanded an equivalent for the crowns which the cities of Greece had at any time offered him in the solemn games. Having forbidden anyone to use the colors of amethyst and Tyrian purple, he privately sent someone to sell a few ounces of them on the day of the Nundinae, and then shut up all the merchants' shops on the pretext that his edict had been violated. It is said that as he was playing and singing in the theater, he observed a married lady dressed in the purple which he had prohibited; he pointed her out to his procurators, upon which she was immediately dragged out of her seat and not only stripped of her clothes, but also her property. He never nominated a person to any office without saying to him, "You know what I want: and let us take care that nobody has anything he can call his own." Finally, he rifled many temples of the rich offerings with which they were furnished, and melted down all the gold and silver statues, amongst them those of the penates, which Galba afterwards restored.

XXXIII.   He began the practice of parricide and murder with Claudius himself, for although he was not the contriver of his death, he was privy to the plot. Nor did he make any secret of it, but used afterwards to commend, in a Greek proverb, mushrooms as food fit for the gods, because Claudius had been poisoned with them. He traduced his memory, both by word and deed, in the grossest manner; one while charging him with folly, another while with cruelty. For he used to say, by way of jest, that he had ceased *morari* amongst men, pronouncing the first syllable long; and treated as null many of his decrees and ordinances as having been made by a doting old blockhead. He enclosed the place where his body was burned with only a low wall of rough masonry. He attempted to poison Britannicus, as much out of envy because he had a sweeter voice as from apprehension of what might ensue from the respect which the people entertained for his father's memory. He employed for this purpose a woman named Locusta who had been a witness against some persons guilty of like practices. But the poison she gave him worked more slowly than he expected and only caused a purge, so he sent for the woman and beat her with his own hand, charging her with administering an antidote instead of poison; and upon her alleging, in excuse, that she had given Britannicus but a gentle mixture in order to prevent suspicion, "Think you," said he, "that I am afraid of the Julian law," and obliged her to prepare, in his own chamber and before his own eyes, as quick and strong a dose as possible. This he tried upon a kid, but as the animal lingered for five hours before it expired he ordered her to go to work again; and when she had done, he gave the poison to a slave, who died immediately. He then commanded the poison to be brought into the eating-room and given to Britannicus, while he was at supper with him. The prince had no sooner tasted it than he sank on the floor, Nero meanwhile pretending to the guests that it was only a fit of the falling sickness, to which, he said, he was subject. He buried him the following day, in a mean and hurried way, during violent storms of rain. He gave Locusta a pardon, and rewarded her with a great estate in land, placing some disciples with her to be instructed in her trade.

XXXIV.   His mother was used to making strict inquiry into what he said or did, and to reprimanding him with the freedom of a parent; he was so much offended by this that he endeavored to expose her to public resentment, by frequently pretending a resolution to quit the government and retire to Rhodes. Soon afterwards, he deprived her of all honor and power, took from her the guard of Roman and German soldiers, banished her from the palace and from his society, and persecuted her in every way he could contrive: employing persons to harass her when at Rome with law-suits, and to disturb her in her retirement from town with the most scurrilous and abusive language, following her about by land and sea. But being terrified by her menaces and violent spirit, he resolved upon her destruction, and thrice attempted it by poison. Finding, however, that she had previously secured herself against this by antidotes, he contrived machinery by which the floor over her bedchamber might be made to fall upon her while she was asleep in the night. This design miscarrying likewise, through the little caution used by those who were in on the secret, his next stratagem was to construct a ship which could be easily shivered, in hopes of destroying her either by drowning, or by the deck above her cabin crushing her in its fall. Accordingly, under the banner of a pretended reconciliation, he wrote her an extremely affectionate letter, inviting her to Baiae to celebrate with him the festival of Minerva. He had given private orders to the captains of the galleys which were to attend her, to shatter to pieces the ship in which she had come, by falling foul of it, but in such a manner that it might appear to be done accidentally. He prolonged the entertainment for the more convenient opportunity of executing the plot in the night; and at her return for Bauli, instead of the old ship which had conveyed her to Baiae, he offered that which he had contrived for her destruction. He attended her to the vessel in a very cheerful mood, and, at parting with her, kissed her breasts, after which he sat up very late in the night, waiting with great anxiety to learn the issue of his project. But receiving information that everything had fallen out contrary to his wish, and that she had saved herself by swimming, not knowing what course to take, upon her freedman, Lucius Agerinus, bringing word, with great joy, that she was safe and well, he privately dropped a poniard by him. He then commanded the freedman to be seized and put in chains, under pretence of his having been employed by his mother to assassinate him; at the same time ordering her to be put to death, and giving out that, to avoid punishment for her intended crime, she had laid violent hands upon herself. Other circumstances, still more horrible, are related on good authority; such as that he went to view her corpse, and, on handling her limbs, pointed out some blemishes and commended other points; and that, growing thirsty during the survey, he called for drink. Yet he was never afterwards able to bear the stings of his own conscience for this atrocious act, although encouraged by the congratulatory addresses of the army, the Senate, and people. He frequently affirmed that he was haunted by his mother's ghost, and persecuted with the whips and burning torches of the Furies. Nay, he attempted by magical rites to bring up her ghost from below, and soften her rage against him. When he was in Greece, he dared not attend the celebration of the Eleusinian mysteries, at the initiation of which impious and wicked persons are warned by the voice of the herald from approaching the rites. Besides the murder of his mother, he had been guilty of that of his aunt; for, being obliged to keep to her bed in consequence of a complaint in her bowels, he paid her a visit, and she, being then advanced in years, stroking his downy chin, in the tenderness of affection, said to him: "May I but live to see the day when this is shaved for the first time, and I shall then die contented." He turned, however, to those about him, made a jest of it, saying that he would have his beard immediately taken off; and ordered the physicians to give her more violent purgatives. He seized upon her estate before she had expired, suppressing her will in order that he might enjoy the whole himself.

XXXV. He had, besides Octavia, two other wives: Poppaea Sabina, whose father had borne the office of quaestor, and who had been married before to a Roman knight; and, after her, Statilia Messalina, great-granddaughter of Taurus, who was twice consul, and received the honor of a triumph. To obtain possession of her, he put to death her husband, Atticus Vestinus, who was then consul. He soon became disgusted with Octavia, and ceased from having any intercourse with her; when censured by his friends for it, he replied, "She ought to be satisfied with having the rank and appendages of his wife." Soon afterwards, he made several attempts, but in vain, to strangle her, and then divorced her for barrenness. But when the people, who disapproved of the divorce, made severe comments on it, he also banished her. In the end he put her to death, upon a charge of adultery so impudent and false that, when all those who were put to the torture positively denied their knowledge of it, he suborned his pedagogue, Anicetus, to affirm that he had secretly intrigued with and debauched her. He married Poppaea twelve days after the divorce of

Octavia, and entertained a great affection for her; but, nevertheless, killed her with a kick which he gave her when she was big with child and in bad health, just because she found fault with him for returning late from driving his chariot. He had by her a daughter, Claudia Augusta, who died an infant. There was no person at all connected with him who escaped his deadly and unjust cruelty. Under pretence of her being engaged in a plot against him, he put to death Antonia, Claudius' daughter, who refused to marry him after the death of Poppaea. In the same way, he destroyed all who were allied to him either by blood or marriage, amongst whom was young Aulus Plautinus. He first compelled him to submit to his unnatural lust, and then ordered him to be executed, crying out, "Let my mother bestow her kisses on my successor thus defiled," pretending that he had been his mother's paramour, and encouraged by her to aspire to the empire. His stepson, Rufinus Crispinus, Poppaea's son, though a minor, he ordered to be drowned in the sea, while he was fishing, by his own slaves, because he was reported to act frequently amongst his playfellows the part of a general or an emperor. He banished Tuscus, his nurse's son, for presuming, when he was procurator of Egypt, to wash in the baths which had been constructed in expectation of his own coming. Seneca, his preceptor, he forced to kill himself, though upon his desiring leave to retire, and offering to surrender his estate, he solemnly swore, "that there was no foundation for his suspicions, and that he would perish himself sooner than hurt him." Having promised Burrus, the praetorian prefect, a remedy for a swelling in his throat, he sent him poison. Some old rich freedmen of Claudius, who had formerly not only promoted his adoption but were also instrumental to his advancement to the empire, and had been his governors, he disposed of by poison given them in their meat or drink.

XXXVI. Nor did he proceed with less cruelty against those who were not of his family. A blazing star, which is vulgarly supposed to portend destruction to kings and princes, appeared above the horizon several nights in succession. He felt great anxiety on account of this phenomenon, as he was informed by one Babilus, an astrologer, that princes used to expiate such omens by the sacrifice of illustrious persons, and so avert the danger foreboded to their own persons by bringing it on the heads of their chief men; he therefore resolved on the destruction of the principal nobility in Rome. He was the more encouraged to do this because he had some plausible pretence for carrying it into execution, from the discovery of two conspiracies against him: the former and more dangerous was that formed by Piso and discovered at Rome; the other was that of Vinicianus, at Beneventum. The conspirators were brought to their trials loaded with triple fetters. Some ingenuously confessed the charge; others avowed that they thought the design against his life an act of favor for which he was obliged to them, as it was impossible in any other way than by death to relieve a person rendered infamous by crimes of the greatest enormity. The children of those who had been condemned were banished from the city, and afterwards either poisoned or starved to death. It is asserted that some of them, with their tutors, and the slaves who carried their satchels, were all poisoned together at one dinner, and others not suffered to seek their daily bread.

XXXVII.   From this period he butchered, without distinction or quarter, all whom his caprice suggested as objects for his cruelty, and upon the most frivolous pretences. To mention only a few: Salvidienus Orfitus was accused of letting out three taverns attached to his house in the forum to some cities for the use of their deputies at Rome. The charge against Cassius Longinus, a lawyer who had lost his sight, was that he kept amongst the busts of his ancestors that of Caius Cassius, who was involved in the death of Julius Caesar. The only charge objected against Paetus Thrasea was that he had a melancholy cast of features, and looked like a schoolmaster. He allowed but one hour to those whom he obliged to kill themselves; and, to prevent delay, he sent them physicians "to *cure* them immediately, if they lingered beyond that time," for so he called bleeding them to death. There was at that time an Egyptian of a most voracious appetite, who would digest raw flesh, or anything else that was given him. It was credibly reported that the emperor was extremely desirous of furnishing him with living men to tear and devour. Being elated with his great success in the perpetration of crimes, he declared "that no prince before himself ever knew the extent of his power." He threw out strong intimations that he would not even spare the senators who survived, but would entirely extirpate that order, and put the provinces and armies into the hands of the Roman knights and his own freedmen. It is certain that he never gave or vouchsafed to allow anyone the customary kiss, either on entering or departing, or even returned a salute. And at the inauguration of a work, the cut through the isthmus, he, with a loud voice, amidst the assembled multitude, uttered a prayer that "the undertaking might prove fortunate for himself and the Roman people," without taking the smallest notice of the Senate.

XXXVIII.   He spared, moreover, neither the people of Rome, nor the capital of the country. Somebody in conversation saying:

emou thanontos gaia michthêtô puri
[When I am dead let fire devour the world]

"Nay," said he, "let it be while I am living" [emou zôntos]. And he acted accordingly, for, pretending to be disgusted with the old buildings, and the streets, he set the city on fire so openly that many of consular rank caught his own household servants on their property with tow, and torches in their hands, but dared not meddle with them. Near his Golden House were some granaries, the site of which he exceedingly coveted; they were battered as if with machines of war, and set on fire, the walls being built of stone. During six days and seven nights this terrible devastation continued, the people being obliged to fly to the tombs and monuments for lodging and shelter. Meanwhile, a vast number of stately buildings, the houses of generals celebrated in former times, and even then still decorated with the spoils of war, were reduced to ashes, as well as the temples of the gods, which had been vowed and dedicated by the kings of Rome, and afterwards in the Punic and Gallic wars: in short, everything that was remarkable and worthy to be seen which time had spared. This fire he beheld from a tower in the house of Maecenas, and, "being greatly delighted," as he said, "with the beautiful effects of the conflagration," he sang a poem on the ruin of Troy, in the tragic dress he used on the stage. To turn this calamity to his own advantage by plunder and rapine, he promised to remove the bodies of those who had perished in the fire, and clear the rubbish at his own expense, suffering no one to meddle with the remains of their property. But he not only received, but exacted contributions on account of the loss, until he had exhausted the means both of the provinces and of private persons.

XXXIX. To these terrible and shameful calamities brought upon the people by their prince were added some proceeding from misfortune. Such were a pestilence, by which, within the space of one autumn, there died no fewer than thirty thousand persons, as appeared from the registers in the temple of Libitina; a great disaster in Britain, where two of the principal towns belonging to the Romans were plundered, and a dreadful havoc made both amongst our troops and allies; a shameful discomfiture of the army of the East, where, in Armenia, the legions were obliged to pass under the yoke, and it was with great difficulty that Syria was retained. Amidst all these disasters, it was strange and, indeed, particularly remarkable that he bore nothing more patiently than the scurrilous language and railing abuse which was in everyone's mouth, treating no class of persons with more gentleness than those who assailed him with invective and lampoons. Many things of that kind were posted up about the city, or otherwise published, both in Greek and Latin: such as these:

> *Nerôn Orestês, Alkmaiôn, mêtroktonoi.*
> *Neonumphon, Nerôn, idian mêter' apekteinen.*

> Orestes and Alcmaon – Nero too,
> The lustful Nero, worst of all the crew,
> Fresh from his bridal – their own mothers slew.

> Quis neget Aeneae magna de stirpe Neronem?
> Sustulit hic matrem: sustulit ille patrem.

> Sprung from Aeneas, pious, wise and great,
> Who says that Nero is degenerate?
> Safe through the flames, one bore his sire; the other,
> To save himself, took off his loving mother.

> Dum tendit citharam noster, dum cornua Parthus,
> Noster erit Peean, ille *hekatêbeletês*

> His lyre to harmony our Nero strings;
> His arrows o'er the plain the Parthian wings:
> Ours call the tuneful Paean, – famed in war,
> The other Phoebus name, the god who shoots afar.

> Roma domus fiet: Vejos migrate, Quirites,
> Si non et Vejos occupat ista domus.

> All Rome will be one house: to Veii fly,
> Should it not stretch to Veii, by and by.

But he neither made any inquiry after the authors, nor when information was laid before the Senate against some of them would he allow a severe sentence to be passed. Isidorus, the Cynic philosopher, said to him aloud, as he was passing along the streets, "You sing the misfortunes of Nauplius well, but behave badly yourself." And Datus, a comic actor, when repeating these words in the piece "Farewell, father! Farewell mother!" mimicked the gestures of persons drinking and swimming, significantly alluding to the deaths of Claudius and Agrippina; and on uttering the last clause,

> Orcus vobus ducit pedes;
> You stand this moment on the brink of Orcus;

he plainly intimated his application of it to the precarious position of the Senate. Yet Nero only banished the player and philosopher from the city and Italy, either because he was insensible to shame, or from apprehension that if he discovered his vexation, still keener things might be said of him.

XL. The world, after tolerating such an emperor for little less than fourteen years, at length forsook him; the Gauls, headed by Julius Vindex, who at that time governed the province as pro-praetor, were the first to revolt. Nero had been formerly told by astrologers that it would be his fortune to be at last deserted by all the world, and this occasioned that celebrated saying of his, "An artist can live in any country," by which he meant to offer as an excuse for his practice of music that it was not only his amusement as a prince, but might be his support when reduced to a private station. Yet some of the astrologers promised him, in his forlorn state, the rule of the East, and in express words the kingdom of Jerusalem. But the greater part of them flattered him with assurances of his being restored to his former fortune. And being most inclined to believe the latter prediction, upon losing Britain and Armenia, he imagined he had run through all his misfortunes which the fates had decreed him. But when, upon consulting the oracle of Apollo at Delphi, he was advised to beware of the seventy-third year, as if he were not to die till then, never thinking of Galba's age, he conceived such hopes not only of living to advanced years, but of constant and singular good fortune, that having lost some things of great value by shipwreck, he did not scruple to say amongst his friends

that "the fishes would bring them back to him." At Naples
he heard of the insurrection in Gaul, on the anniversary of
the day on which he killed his mother, and bore it with so
much unconcern as to excite a suspicion that he was really
glad of it, since he had now a fair opportunity of plundering those wealthy provinces by the right of war. Immediately going to the gymnasium, he witnessed the exercise of
the wrestlers with the greatest delight. Being interrupted
at supper with letters which brought yet worse news, he
expressed no greater resentment than only to threaten
the rebels. For eight days together, he never attempted to
answer any letters, nor give any orders, but buried the whole
affair in profound silence.

XLI. Being roused at last by numerous proclamations
of Vindex, treating him with reproaches and contempt, in a
letter to the Senate he exhorted them to avenge his wrongs
and those of the republic, desiring them to excuse his not
appearing in the senate house because he had got cold. But
nothing so much galled him as to find himself railed at as
a pitiful harpist, and, instead of Nero, styled Ahenobarbus;
this being his family name, since he was upbraided with it,
he declared he would resume it, and lay aside the name he
had taken by adoption. Passing by the other accusations as
wholly groundless, he earnestly refuted that of his want of
skill in an art upon which he had bestowed so much pains,
and in which he had arrived at such perfection, asking
frequently those about him, "if they knew anyone who
was a more accomplished musician?" But being alarmed
by messenger after messenger of ill news from Gaul, he
returned in great consternation to Rome. On the road, his
mind was somewhat relieved by observing the frivolous
omen of a Gaulish soldier defeated and dragged by the hair
by a Roman knight, which was sculptured on a monument; so that he leaped for joy, and adored the heavens.
Even then he made no appeal either to the Senate or people,
but calling together some of the leading men at his own
house, he held a hasty consultation on the present state of

affairs, and then, during the remainder of the day, carried them about with him to view some musical instruments, of a new invention, which were played by water, exhibiting all the parts, and discoursing upon the principles and difficulties of the contrivance which, he told them, he intended to produce in the theater, if Vindex would give him leave.

XLII. Soon afterwards, he received intelligence that Galba and the Spaniards had declared against him, upon which he fainted and, losing his reason, lay a long time speechless, and apparently dead. As soon as he recovered from this state of stupefaction, he tore his clothes and beat his head, crying, "It is all over with me!" His nurse endeavored to comfort him, telling him that similar things had happened to other princes before him; he replied, "I am beyond all example wretched, for I have lost an empire whilst I am still living." He nevertheless abated nothing of his usual luxury and inattention to business. Nay, on the arrival of good news from the provinces, at a sumptuous entertainment he sang with an air of merriment some jovial verses upon the leaders of the revolt, which were made public, and accompanied them with suitable gestures. After being carried privately to the theater, he sent word to an actor who was applauded by the spectators, "that he had it all his own way, now that he himself did not appear on the stage."

XLIII. At the first breaking out of these troubles, it is believed that he had formed many designs of a monstrous nature, although conformable enough to his natural disposition. These were to send new governors and commanders to the provinces and the armies, and employ assassins to butcher all the former governors and commanders, as men unanimously engaged in a conspiracy against him; to massacre the exiles in every quarter, and all the Gaulish population in Rome, the former lest they should join the insurrection, the latter as privy to the designs of their countrymen and ready to support them; to abandon Gaul itself, to be wasted and plundered by his armies; to poison the whole Senate at a feast; to fire the city, and then let loose the wild beasts upon the people, in order to impede their stopping the progress of the flames. But, deterred from the execution of these designs, not so much by remorse of conscience as by despair of being able to effect them, and judging an expedition into Gaul necessary, he removed the consuls from their office, before the time of its expiration had arrived, and in their place assumed the consulship himself without a colleague, as if the fates had decreed that Gaul should not be conquered, except by a consul. Upon assuming the fasces, after an entertainment at the palace, as he walked out of the room leaning on the arms of some of his friends, he declared that as soon as he arrived in the province, he would make his appearance amongst the troops, unarmed, and do nothing but weep; and that, after he had brought the mutineers to repentance, he would, the next day, in the public rejoicings, sing songs of triumph, which he must now, without loss of time, apply himself to compose.

XLIV. In preparing for this expedition, his first care was to provide carriages for his musical instruments and machinery to be used on the stage; to have the hair of the concubines he carried with him dressed in the fashion of men; and to supply them with battle-axes and Amazonian bucklers. He summoned the city-tribes to enlist, but when no qualified persons appeared, he ordered all masters to send a certain number of slaves, the best they had, not excepting their stewards and secretaries. He commanded the several orders of the people to bring in a fixed proportion of their estates, as they stood in the censor's books; all tenants of houses and mansions to pay one year's rent forthwith into the exchequer; and with unheard-of strictness, he would receive only new coin of the purest silver and the finest gold; insomuch that most people refused to pay, crying out unanimously that he ought to squeeze the informers, and oblige them to surrender their gains.

XLV. The general odium in which he was held was increased by the great scarcity of corn, and an occurrence connected with it. For, just at that time, there arrived from Alexandria a ship which was said to be freighted with dust for the wrestlers belonging to the emperor. This so much inflamed the public rage that he was treated with the utmost abuse and scurrility. On the top of one of his statues was placed the figure of a chariot with a Greek inscription that "Now indeed he had a race to run; let him be gone." A little bag was tied about another, with a ticket containing these words: "What could I do?" – "Truly thou hast merited the sack." Some person likewise wrote on the pillars in the Forum "that he had even woke *the cocks* with his singing." And many, in the night-time, pretending to find fault with their servants, frequently called for a *Vindex*.

XLVI. He was also terrified by manifest warnings, both old and new, arising from dreams, auspices, and omens. He had never used to dream before the murder of his mother. After that event, he fancied in his sleep that he was steering a ship, and that the rudder was forced from him: that he was dragged by his wife Octavia into a prodigiously dark place; and was at one time covered over with a vast swarm of winged ants, and at another, surrounded by the national images which were set up near Pompey's theater, and hindered from advancing farther; that a Spanish jennet he was fond of had his hinder parts so changed as to resemble those of an ape and, having his head only left unaltered, neighed very harmoniously. The doors of the mausoleum of Augustus flying open by themselves, there issued from it a voice, calling on him by name. The Lares, being adorned with fresh garlands on the calends (the first) of January, fell down during the preparations for sacrificing to them. While he was taking the omens, Sporus presented him with a ring, the stone of which had carved upon it the Rape of Proserpine. When a great multitude of the several orders was assembled, to attend at the solemnity of making vows to the gods, it was a long time before the keys of the Capitol could be found. And when, in a speech of his to the senate against Vindex, these words were read, "that the miscreants should be punished and soon make the end they merited," they all cried out, "You will do it, Augustus." It was likewise remarked that the last tragic piece which he sang was *Oedipus in Exile,* and that he fell as he was repeating this verse:

> *thanein m' anôige sungamos, mêtêr, patêr.*
> Wife, mother, father, force me to my end.

XLVII.   Meanwhile, on the arrival of the news that the rest of the armies had declared against him, he tore to pieces the letters which were delivered to him at dinner, overthrew the table, and dashed with violence against the ground two favorite cups, which he called Homer's, because some of that poet's verses were engraved upon them. Then taking from Locusta a dose of poison, which he put up in a golden box, he went into the Servilian gardens and thence dispatched a trusty freedman to Ostia, with orders to make ready a fleet; he endeavored to prevail on some tribunes and centurions of the praetorian guards to attend him in his flight; but as some of them showed no great inclination to comply, others absolutely refused, and one of them cried out aloud:

> Usque adeone mori miserum est?
> *Say, is it then so sad a thing to die?*

he was in great perplexity whether he should submit himself to Galba, or apply to the Parthians for protection, or else appear before the people dressed in mourning, and, upon the rostra, in the most piteous manner, beg pardon for his past misdemeanors, and, if he could not prevail, request of them to grant him at least the government of Egypt. A speech to this purpose was afterwards found in his writing-case. But it is conjectured that he dared not venture upon this project, for fear of being torn to pieces before he could get to the forum. Deferring, therefore, his resolution until the next day, he awoke about midnight, and finding the guards withdrawn, he leaped out of bed, and sent round for his friends. But when none of them vouchsafed any message in reply, he went with a few attendants to their houses. As the doors everywhere were shut, and no one was giving him any answer, he returned to his bedchamber, whence those who were in charge of it had all now eloped; some having gone one way, and some another, carrying off with them his bedding and box of poison. He then endeavored to find Spicillus, the gladiator, or someone to kill him; but as he was unable to procure any one, "What!" said he, "have I then neither friend nor foe?" he immediately ran out, as if he would throw himself into the Tiber.

XLVIII. But when this furious impulse subsided, he wished for some place of privacy where he might collect his thoughts; and when his freedman Phaon offered him his country-house, between the Salarian and Nomentan roads, about four miles from the city, he mounted a horse, barefoot as he was, and in his tunic, only slipping over it an old soiled cloak, with his head muffled up and a handkerchief before his face, and four persons only to attend him, of whom Sporus was one. He was suddenly struck with horror at an earthquake, and by a flash of lightning which darted full in his face, and heard from the neighboring camp the shouts of the soldiers, wishing his destruction and prosperity to Galba. He also heard a traveler they met on the road say, "They are in pursuit of Nero," and another ask, "Is there any news in the city about Nero?" Uncovering his face when his horse was started by the scent of a carcass which lay in the road, he was recognized and saluted by an old soldier who had been discharged from the guards. When they came to the lane which turned up to the house, they quitted their horses, and with much difficulty he wound among bushes and briars, and along a track through a bed of rushes, over which they spread their cloaks for him to walk on. Having reached a wall at the back of the villa, Phaon advised him to hide himself awhile in a sandpit, but he replied, "I will not go underground alive." Staying there some little time, while preparations were made for bringing him privately into the villa, he took some water out of a neighboring tank in his hand to drink, saying, "This is Nero's distilled water." Then his cloak having been torn by the brambles, he pulled out the thorns which stuck in it. At last, being admitted, creeping upon his hands and knees, through a hole made for him in the wall, he lay down in the first closet he came to, upon a miserable pallet, with an old coverlet thrown over it; and being both hungry and thirsty, though he refused some coarse bread that was brought him, he drank a little warm water.

XLIX. As all who surrounded him were now pressing him to save himself from the indignities which were ready to befall him, he ordered a pit to be sunk before his eyes, of the size of his body, and the bottom to be covered with pieces of marble put together, if any could be found about the house; and water and wood to be got ready for immediate use about his corpse; weeping at everything that was done, and frequently saying, "What an artist is now about to perish!" Meanwhile, when letters were brought in by a servant belonging to Phaon, he snatched them out of his hand, and there read "that he had been declared an enemy by the Senate, and that a search was being made for him, that he might be punished according to the ancient custom of the Romans." He then inquired what kind of punishment that was; and on being told that the practice was to strip the criminal naked and scourge him to death, while his neck was fastened within a forked stake, he was so terrified that he took up two daggers which he had brought with him, and after feeling the points of both, put them up again, saying, "The fatal hour is not yet come." One while, he begged of Sporus to begin to wail and lament; another while, he entreated that one of them would set him an example by killing himself; and then again, he condemned his own want of resolution in these words: "I yet live to my shame and disgrace: this is not becoming for Nero: it is not becoming. Thou oughtest in such circumstances to have a good heart: Come, then: courage, man!" The horsemen, who had received orders to bring him away alive, were now approaching the house. As soon as he heard them coming, he uttered with a trembling voice the following verse,

> *hippôn m' ôkupodôn amphi ktupos ouata ballei;*
> Il. x. 535.
> The noise of swift-heel'd steeds assails my ears;

and drove a dagger into his throat, being assisted in the act by Epaphroditus, his secretary. To a centurion who burst in just as he was half-dead, and applied his cloak to the wound, pretending that he had come to his assistance, he made no other reply but this, "'Tis too late" and "Is this your loyalty?" Immediately after pronouncing these words he expired, with his eyes fixed and starting out of his head, to the terror of all who beheld him. He had requested of his attendants, as the most essential favor, that they would let no one have his head, but that by all means his body might be burned entire. And this, Icelus, Galba's freedman, granted. He had but a little before been discharged from the prison into which he had been thrown, when the disturbances first broke out.

L. The expenses of his funeral amounted to two hundred thousand sesterces; the bed upon which his body was carried to the pile and burned was covered with the white robes, interwoven with gold, which he had worn upon the calends of January preceding. His nurses, Ecloge and Alexandria, with his concubine Acte, deposited his remains in the tomb belonging to the family of the Domitii, which stands on the top of the Hill of the Gardens, and is to be seen from the Campus Martius. In that monument, a coffin of porphyry, with an altar of marble of Luna over it, is enclosed by a wall built of stone brought from Thasos.

LI.   In stature he was a little below the common height; his skin was foul and spotted; his hair inclined to yellow; his features were agreeable rather than handsome; his eyes grey and dull, his neck was thick, his belly prominent, his legs very slender, his constitution sound. For, though excessively luxurious in his mode of living, he had, in the course of fourteen years, only three fits of sickness, which were so slight that he neither forbore the use of wine nor made any alteration in his usual diet. In his dress and the care of his person he was so careless that he had his hair cut in rings, one above another; and when in Achaea he let it grow long behind; and he generally appeared in public in the loose dress which he used at table, with a handkerchief about his neck, and without either a girdle or shoes.

LII.   He was instructed, when a boy, in the rudiments of almost all the liberal sciences, but his mother diverted him from the study of philosophy, as unsuited to one destined to be an emperor; and his preceptor, Seneca, discouraged him from reading the ancient orators, that he might longer secure his devotion to himself. Therefore, having a turn for poetry, he composed verses both with pleasure and ease; nor did he, as some think, publish those of other writers as his own. Several little pocketbooks and loose sheets have come into my possession, which contain some well-known verses in his own hand, and written in such a manner that it was very evident, from the blotting and interlining, that they had not been transcribed from a copy, nor dictated by another, but were written by the composer of them.

LIII.   He had likewise great taste for drawing and painting, as well as for molding statues in plaster. But, above all things, he most eagerly coveted popularity, being the rival of every man who obtained the applause of the people for anything he did. It was the general belief that, after the crowns he won by his performances on the stage, he would the next lustrum have taken his place among the wrestlers at the Olympic games. For he was continually practicing that art; nor did he witness the gymnastic games in any part of Greece otherwise than sitting on the ground in the stadium, as the umpires do. And if a pair of wrestlers happened to break the bounds, he would drag them back into the center of the circle with his own hands. Because he was thought to equal Apollo in music, and the sun in chariot-driving, he resolved also to imitate the achievements of Hercules. And they say that a lion was got ready for him to kill, either with a club or with a close hug, in view of the people in the amphitheater, which he was to perform naked.

LIV. Towards the end of his life, he publicly vowed that if his power in the state was securely reestablished, he would, in the spectacles which he intended to exhibit in honor of his success, include a performance upon organs, as well as upon flutes and bagpipes, and, on the last day of the games, would act in the play and take the part of Turnus, as we find it in Virgil. And there are some who say that he put to death the player Paris as a dangerous rival.

LV. He had an insatiable desire to immortalize his name, and acquire a reputation which should last through all succeeding ages, but it was capriciously directed. He therefore took from several things and places their former appellations, and gave them new names derived from his own. He called the month of April, Neroneus, and designed changing the name of Rome to that of Neropolis.

LVI. He held all religious rites in contempt, except those of the Syrian Goddess; but at last he paid her so little reverence that he made water upon her, as he was now engaged in another superstition, in which only he obstinately persisted. For having received from some obscure plebeian a little image of a girl, as a preservative against plots, and discovering a conspiracy immediately after, he constantly worshipped his imaginary protectress as the greatest amongst the gods, offering to her three sacrifices daily. He was also desirous to have it supposed that he had, by revelations from this deity, a knowledge of future events. A few months before he died, he attended a sacrifice, according to the Etruscan rites, but the omens were not favorable.

LVII.   He died in the thirty-second year of his age, upon the same day on which he had formerly put Octavia to death; and the public joy was so great upon the occasion that the common people ran about the city with caps upon their heads. Some, however, were not wanting, who for a long time decked his tomb with spring and summer flowers. Sometimes they placed his image upon the rostra, dressed in robes of state; at another, they published proclamations in his name, as if he were still alive and would shortly return to Rome, and take vengeance on all his enemies. Vologesus, king of the Parthians, when he sent ambassadors to the Senate to renew his alliance with the Roman people, earnestly requested that due honor should be paid to the memory of Nero; and, to conclude, when, twenty years afterwards, at which time I was a young man, some person of obscure birth gave himself out for Nero, that name secured for him so favorable a reception from the Parthians that he was very zealously supported, and it was with much difficulty that they were prevailed upon to give him up.

Remarks on Nero

Though no law had ever been passed for regulating the transmission of the imperial power, yet the design of conveying it by lineal descent was implied in the practice of adoption. By the rule of hereditary succession, Britannicus, the son of Claudius, was the natural heir to the throne; but he was supplanted by the artifices of his stepmother, who had the address to procure it for her own son, Nero. From the time of Augustus it had been the custom of each of the new sovereigns to commence his reign in such a manner as tended to acquire popularity, however much they all afterwards degenerated from those specious beginnings. Whether this proceeded entirely from policy, or that nature was not yet vitiated by the intoxication of uncontrolled power, is uncertain; but such were the excesses into which they afterwards plunged that we can scarcely exempt any of them, except, perhaps, Claudius, from the imputation of great original depravity. The vicious temper of Tiberius was known to his own mother, Livia; that of Caligula had been obvious to those about him from his infancy; Claudius seems to have had naturally a stronger tendency to weakness than to vice; but the inherent wickedness of Nero was discovered at an early period by his preceptor, Seneca. Yet even this emperor commenced his reign in a manner which procured him approbation. Of all the Roman emperors who had hitherto reigned, he seems to have been most corrupted by profligate favorites, who flattered his follies and vices to promote their own aggrandizement. Among these was Tigellinus, who met at last with the fate which he had so amply merited.

The several reigns from the death of Augustus present us with uncommon scenes of cruelty and horror; but it was reserved for that of Nero to exhibit to the world the atrocious act of an emperor deliberately procuring the death of his mother.

Julia Agrippina was the daughter of Germanicus, and married Domitius Ahenobarbus, by whom she had Nero. At the death of Messalina she was a widow; when Claudius, her uncle, entertained a design of entering again into the married state, she aspired to an incestuous alliance with him, in competition with Lollia Paulina, a woman of beauty and intrigue, who had been married to C. Caesar. The two rivals were strongly supported by their respective parties;

but Agrippina, by her superior interest with the emperor's favorites, and the familiarity to which her near relations gave her a claim, obtained the preference; and the portentous nuptials of the emperor and his niece were publicly solemnized in the palace. Whether she was prompted to this flagrant indecency by personal ambition alone, or by the desire of procuring the succession to the empire for her son, is uncertain; but there remains no doubt of her having removed Claudius by poison, with a view to the object now mentioned. Besides Claudius, she projected the death of L. Silanus, and she accomplished that of his brother Junius Silanus, by means likewise of poison. She appears to have been richly endowed with the gifts of nature, but in her disposition intriguing, violent, imperious, and ready to sacrifice every principle of virtue in the pursuit of supreme power or sensual gratification. As she resembled Livia in the ambition of a mother, and the means by which she indulged it, so she more than equaled her in the ingratitude of an unnatural son and a parricide. She is said to have left behind her some memoirs, of which Tacitus availed himself in the composition of his Annals.

In this reign, the conquest of the Britons still continued to be the principal object of military enterprise, and Suetonius Paulinus was invested with the command of the Roman army employed in the reduction of that people. The island of Mona, now Anglesey, being the chief seat of the Druids, he resolved to commence his operations with attacking a place which was the center of superstition, and to which the vanquished Britons retreated as the last asylum of liberty. The inhabitants endeavored, both by force of arms and the terrors of religion, to obstruct his landing on this sacred island. The women and Druids assembled promiscuously with the soldiers on the shore, where, running about in wild disorder, with flaming torches in their hands, and pouring forth the most hideous exclamations, they struck the Romans with consternation. But Suetonius animated his troops, and they boldly attacked the inhabitants, routed them in the field, and burned the Druids in the same fires which had been prepared by those priests for the catastrophe of the invaders, destroying at the same time all the consecrated graves and altars in the island. Suetonius, having thus triumphed over the religion of the Britons, flattered himself with the hopes of soon effecting the reduction of the people. But they, encouraged by his absence, had taken arms, and under the conduct of Boudicca, queen of the Iceni, who had been treated in the most ignominious manner by the Roman tribunes, had already driven the haughty invaders from their several settlements. Suetonius hastened to the protection of London, which was by this time a flourishing Roman colony; but he found, upon his arrival, that any attempt to preserve it would be attended with the utmost danger to the army. London therefore was reduced to ashes; and the Romans, and all strangers, to the number of seventy thousand, were put to the sword without distinction, the Britons seeming determined to convince the enemy that they would acquiesce in no other terms than a total evacuation of the island. This massacre, however, was revenged by Suetonius in a decisive engagement, where eighty thousand of the Britons are said to have been killed; after which, Boudicca, to avoid falling into the hands of the insolent conquerors, put an end to her own life by means of poison. It being judged unadvisable that Suetonius should any longer conduct the war against a people whom he had exasperated by his severity, he was recalled, and Petronius Turpilianus appointed in his place. The command was afterwards given successively to Trebellius Maximus and Vettius Bolanus, but the plan pursued by these generals was only to retain, by a conciliatory administration, the parts of the island which had already submitted to the Roman arms.

During these transactions in Britain, Nero himself was exhibiting, in Rome or some of the provinces, such scenes of extravagance as almost exceed credibility. In one place, entering the lists amongst the competitors in a chariot race; in another contending for victory with the common musicians on the stage; reveling in open day in the company of the most abandoned prostitutes and the vilest of men; in the night, committing depredations on the peaceful inhabitants of the capital; polluting with detestable lust, or drenching with human blood, the streets, the palaces, and the habitations of private families; and, to crown his enormities, setting fire to Rome, while he sang with delight in beholding the dreadful conflagration. In vain would history be ransacked for a parallel to this emperor, who united the most shameful vices to the most extravagant vanity, the most abject meanness to the strongest but most preposterous ambition; and the whole of whose life was one continued scene of lewdness, sensuality, rapine, cruelty, and folly. It is emphatically observed by Tacitus "that Nero, after the murder of many illustrious personages, manifested a desire of extirpating virtue itself."

Among other excesses of Nero's reign are to be mentioned the horrible cruelties exercised against the Christians in various parts of the empire, in which inhuman transactions the natural barbarity of the emperor was inflamed by the prejudices and interested policy of the pagan priesthood.

The tyrant did not scruple to charge them with the act of burning Rome, and he satiated his fury against them by such outrages as are unexampled in history. They were covered with the skins of wild beasts and torn by dogs; were crucified, and set on fire, that they might serve for lights in the night-time. Nero offered his garden for this spectacle, and exhibited the games of the Circus by this dreadful illumination. Sometimes they were covered with wax and other combustible materials, after which a sharp stake was put under their chin, to make them stand upright, and they were burned alive, to give light to the spectators.

In the person of Nero, it is observed by Suetonius, the race of the Caesars became extinct; a race rendered illustrious by the first and second emperors, but which their successors no less disgraced. The despotism of Julius Caesar, though haughty and imperious, was liberal and humane;

that of Augustus, if we exclude a few instances of vindictive severity toward individuals, was mild and conciliating; but the reigns of Tiberius, Caligula, and Nero (for we except Claudius from part of the censure), while discriminated from each other by some peculiar circumstances, exhibited the most flagrant acts of licentiousness and perverted authority. The most abominable lust, the most extravagant luxury, the most shameful rapaciousness, and the most inhuman cruelty constitute the general characteristics of those capricious and detestable tyrants. Repeated experience now clearly refuted the opinion of Augustus, that he had introduced amongst the Romans the best form of government; but while we make this observation, it is proper to remark that, had he even restored the republic, there is reason to believe that the nation would again have been soon distracted with internal divisions and a perpetual succession of civil wars. The manners of the people had become too dissolute to be restrained by the authority of elective and temporary magistrates, and the Romans were hastening to that fatal period when general and great corruption, with its attendant debility, would render them an easy prey to any foreign invaders.

Bibliography

Barrett, A. A., *Agrippina: Mother of Nero* (London, 1996).

Boethius, A., *The Golden House of Nero* (Ann Arbor, MI, 1960).

Brunt, P. A., "The Revolt of Vindex and the Fall of Nero," *Latomus* 18 (1959), 531–559.

Charlesworth, M. P., "Nero: Some Aspects," *The Journal of Roman Studies* 40 (1950), 69–76.

Christ, K., *Geschichte der römischen Kaiserzeit* (Munich, 1992).

Eck, W., *Agrippina, die Stadtgründerin Kölns* (Cologne, 1993).

——, *The Age of Augustus*, tr. Deborah Lucas Schneider (Oxford, 2002).

Elsner, J., and J. Masters, eds, *Reflections of Nero: Culture, History and Representation* (London, 1994).

Fuhrmann, M., *Seneca und Kaiser Nero. Eine Biographie* (Berlin, 1997).

Grant, M., *Nero* (London, 1970).

Griffin, M., *Nero: The End of a Dynasty* (London, 1984).

——, *Seneca: A Philosopher in Politics* (Oxford, 1976).

Heil, M., *Die orientalische Außenpolitik des Kaisers Nero* (Munich, 1997).

Henderson, B. W., *The Life and Principate of the Emperor Nero* [London, 1905] (repr. Rome, 1968).

Kierdorf, W., *Sueton, Leben des Claudius und Nero* (Paderborn etc., 1992).

Murray, O., "The 'quinquennium Neronis' and the Stoics," *Historia* 14 (1965), 41–61.

Rilinger, R., "Seneca und Nero. Konzepte zur Legitimation kaiserlicher Herrschaft," *Klio* 78, no. 1 (1996), 130–157.

Rogers, R. S., "Heirs and Rivals to Nero," *Transactions and Proceedings of the American Philological Association* 86 (1955), 190–212.

Rudich, V., *Political Dissidence under Nero: The Price of Dissimulation* (London, 1993).

Schubert, C., *Studien zum Nerobild in der lateinischen Dichtung der Antike* (Stuttgart and Leipzig, 1998).

Shotter, D., *Nero* (London, 1996).

Walter, G., *Nero*, tr. Emma Craufurd (London, 1957).

Warmington, B. H., *Nero: Reality and Legend* (London, 1969).

Weege, F., "Das Goldene Haus des Nero," *Jahrbuch des Kaiserlich Deutschen Archäologischen Instituts* 28 (1913), 127–244.

Wiedemann, T., *The Julio-Claudian Emperors* (Bristol, 1989).

Two literary depictions of Nero and the history of his time deserve special mention: the 1896 novel, *Quo Vadis*, by Henryk Sienkiewicz, tr. W. S. Kuniczak (New York, 1997) and *The Pretender*, a novel by Lion Feuchtwanger, tr. Willa and Edwin Muir (New York, 1937).

Index

Note: References in *italics* denote illustrations.